Going Places

Going Places

How America's Best and Brightest Got Started Down the Road of Life

E. D. HILL

ReganBooks

An Imprint of HarperCollins*Publishers*

Photography Credits

Page 3 by Kristin Barlowe, courtesy of Milam Music Group; page 16 by Ray Amati; page 32 courtesy of DeMatha Catholic High School; page 39 courtesy of the White House; page 42 courtesy of Princeton University; page 46 courtesy of the U.S. Department of Labor; page 52 courtesy of Ted Baehr; pages 57, 176, and 280 courtesy of the U.S. Senate; page 62 by Mark Garten/UN Photo; page 72 by Bruce Plotkin; page 84 courtesy of Alpha Press; page 97 courtesy of the U.S. House of Representatives; page 101 by Paul Harris/Getty Images; page 111 courtesy of Lambchop Productions; page 115 courtesy of the U.S. Department of Justice; page 124 courtesy of the U.S. Department of State; page 138 courtesy of the U.S. Department of Housing and Urban Development; page 145 courtesy of BET; page 153 Stan Honda/AFP/Getty Images; page 158 courtesy of BeFit Enterprises; page 169 by Beiron Andersson/PBR; page 180 by Frank Veronsky; page 186 by Frazer Harrison/Getty Images; page 191 by Stuart Ramson, courtesy of Xerox Corporation; page 199 by Eric A. Amundson; page 203 courtesy of News Corporation; page 207 by Robert Mora/Getty Images; page 219 by Dennis Carney; page 222 courtesy of the Westchester County (NY) District Attorney's Office; page 227 by Kim Jew Photography; page 247 by Curtis McElhinney, www.curtisvision.com; page 256 courtesy of Lucent Technologies; page 260 courtesy of Rich Clarkson and Associates; pages 265 and 271 courtesy of the Charles Bush Studio; page 268 courtesy of CBS News; all other photos are courtesy of the contributors.

HarperCollins books may be purchased for educational, business, or sales promotional use. For information please write: Special Markets Department, HarperCollins Publishers Inc., 10 East 53rd Street, New York, NY 10022.

FIRST EDITION

Designed by Kris Tobiasson

Printed on acid-free paper

Library of Congress Cataloging-in-Publication Data has been applied for.

ISBN 10: 0-06-082804-8
ISBN 13: 978-0-06-082804-2

05 06 07 08 09 WBC/RRD 10 9 8 7 6 5 4 3 2 1

To the loves of my life, my husband, Joe, and our children, Jordan, Laurel, Matt, Collin, J. D., Wyatt, Sumner, and Wolf. To my parents, Joan and W. H. "Bill" Tarbox, for unconditional love. To my in-laws, Delores and John and Joan and Sandy, for their incredible support.

CONTENTS

INTRODUCTION 1

TRACE ADKINS 3

DR. ARTHUR AGATSTON 7

SENATOR GEORGE ALLEN 11

CAROL ALT 16

DENISE AUSTIN 21

TIKI BARBER 26

JAMES "J. B." BROWN 32

PRESIDENT GEORGE W. BUSH 39

DEAN CAIN 42

SECRETARY OF LABOR ELAINE L. CHAO 46

SENATOR NORM COLEMAN 52

SENATOR JON CORZINE 57

SENATOR JOHN DANFORTH 62

DONNA DE VARONA 67

BASH DIBRA 72

STEVE DOOCY 76

EMME 79

SARAH FERGUSON, THE DUCHESS OF YORK 84

GERALDINE FERRARO 89

STEVE FORBES 93

REPRESENTATIVE HAROLD FORD JR. 97

GEORGE FOREMAN 101

SENATOR WILLIAM FRIST 105

KATHIE LEE GIFFORD 111

ATTORNEY GENERAL ALBERTO GONZALES 115

ROSEY GRIER 119

SECRETARY OF STATE ALEXANDER HAIG 124

REBECCA HUFFMAN 128

SENATOR KAY BAILEY HUTCHISON 132

RANDY JACKSON 136

SECRETARY ALPHONSO JACKSON 138

BOB JOHNSON 145

JIM KEYES 149

DR. HENRY KISSINGER 153

JACK LaLANNE 158

SECRETARY OF THE NAVY JOHN LEHMAN 164

JUSTIN McBRIDE 169

JOHN MACK 172

SENATOR MEL MARTINEZ 176

MARY MEEKER 180

SENATOR ZELL MILLER 182

RONNIE MILSAP 186

ANNE MULCAHY 191

COLONEL OLIVER NORTH 194

TED NUGENT 199

BILL O'REILLY 203

DONNY OSMOND 207

RANDY OWEN 210

DR. MEHMET OZ 214

DOLLY PARTON 219

DISTRICT ATTORNEY JEANINE PIRRO 222

GOVERNOR BILL RICHARDSON 227

CATHY RIGBY 231

GERALDO RIVERA 236

DORIS ROBERTS 241

KENNY ROGERS 243

MICKEY AND JAN ROONEY 247

SECRETARY OF DEFENSE DONALD RUMSFELD 251

PATRICIA F. RUSSO 256

REPRESENTATIVE JIM RYUN 260

CONNIE SELLECCA 265

HANNAH STORM 268

JOHN TESH 271

JOE THEISMANN 275

SENATOR FRED THOMPSON 280

JONATHAN TISCH 284

DONALD TRUMP 288

SANDY WEILL 292

HENRY WINKLER 297

ME (E. D. HILL) 301

ACKNOWLEDGMENTS 307

Going Places

INTRODUCTION

My oldest child just became a teenager. It's that dreaded time in every parent's life that's marked by daily battles over what clothes they wear, what TV shows they watch, what music they listen to, and which people influence their lives. A while back, I decided that I wanted to make time every evening to read with my children. Well, what sounded like a nice idea ended up turning into the biggest battle of all. While I wanted to read adventure books about great explorers like Lewis and Clark, my twelve-year-old son was only interested in NFL scouting magazines. My thirteen-year-old daughter couldn't tear herself away from romance novels (which are far steamier than they used to be!), and my nine-year-old just wanted to read the same shark book over and over and over.

Taking in my family's eclectic tastes, I decided that instead of trying to pick one book that would please us all, we would instead use reading time as an opportunity to discuss inspirational, honorable, successful, or just plain interesting people in the world.

While searching the bookstore, I found plenty of motivational advice books and biographies of leaders, but none of them really seemed right for my kids. I was searching for a book that would inspire, educate, and entertain. Plus, I wanted something that would captivate my teenager without going over the heads of my little ones. Through my job hosting *Fox and Friends* on the Fox News Channel, I am constantly meeting people who inspire me. One night, I was telling my boys about meeting David Robinson, a Naval Academy graduate known as the "Admiral" of the San Antonio Spurs, who had been on the show that morning. For the first three years in high school, David tried out for the basketball team and was rejected because he was too short. Then, during the summer between his junior and senior years, he grew six inches—and that fall, finally, he made the team. Later on, at the Naval Academy, he grew seven more inches and became a two-time All-American winner. As a pro ballplayer, David ended up being named the NBA Rookie of the Year and the League MVP.

On the show, I asked him if his added height had made all the difference to his game. To my surprise, he said no. What really mattered, he told me, was the advice his mother gave him in high school. "You can achieve anything," she had told him. "But you have to work toward your goal, expecting to reach it." That was why, although he didn't make the team early on, David had spent his time memorizing the plays, learning the strategies, and practicing his shots. By the time he reached his goal and made the team, he was ready to play at full speed.

Keeping this story in mind, I began asking people to share the pieces of advice that made a difference in their lives, careers, or priorities. I was amazed by their answers. I realized that their stories not only fascinated me, but would be interesting and inspirational to my children. With that, the idea for the book was born.

For this collection, I've deliberately chosen people from all walks of life. But the lessons they shared with me are universal. It is my hope that you'll have this book by your bedside table and turn to it, alone or with your children, to find inspiration from wonderful people. With luck, their thoughts and insights could be just the advice you've been looking for on your own path to success.

TRACE ADKINS

COUNTRY MUSIC SINGER

Trace Adkins, a six-foot-six, 250-pound former gospel singer, stands out in a crowd. When you meet him, you're struck at once by how immense he is—yet his sensitivity is impossible to miss. You immediately feel you know him. Perhaps it's because he's a lot like you. He's had his ups and downs and then some. He's been married, divorced, married, divorced, and married again, this time happily at last. He talks about his children and asks you about yours. He worries about the impact of broken homes.

Trace took a while to find himself. At Louisiana Tech he played football and studied both music and petroleum technology, which ultimately led to a job working on oil rigs. But when he finally got a break in Nashville, his music career took off.

The songs Trace sings are honest and open. Through them, you see the man he is.

GO WHERE THE FACTORY IS
AND GET IN THE GAME

I'd been playing clubs in Texas for about four years and I had pretty much given up hope. I was burned out on the whole scene. I just thought, "Well, it's not going to happen for me." I'd been under the impression that somebody was going to see me playing in one of those little clubs and say, "Come here. I want to make you a star." It never happened, and I got frustrated. So I spent the next three years working in the oil fields.

I truly enjoyed the work. I liked the camaraderie and the machismo of the whole thing. It's a hard-core world out in the oil field, working on the drilling rigs, and I liked it. Then one day, out of the blue, the guy who had been booking me in those clubs called me on the phone to ask if I was singing anymore. I told him no. He said, "Well, that's unfortunate. One of these days you're going to have to look at yourself in the mirror and ask yourself the question, I wonder what would've happened if . . . ?" I told him, "I just couldn't take it anymore, man." And he replied, "That's not what I'm talking about. I mean that if you really want it, you've got to throw down the pom-poms. Go where the factory is and get in the game. Get yourself to Nashville."

I hung up the phone and really thought about what he'd said. The prospect of moving was kind of scary. I wasn't sure I really wanted to leave the only home I'd ever known. But you know what? The thought of me being sixty-five years old, looking in the mirror, and asking myself that question scared me worse. John Milam was his name. I will always be indebted to him and I'll never forget him for that.

For some people, success finds them, but that's the exception rather than the rule. I knew that Nashville is where singers become stars. And I knew that John was right. It took his shaking me up like that and making me take a good hard look at myself to give me the courage to take the step. I decided that I would try out Nashville for three or four years, and if it didn't happen I would still be in good enough physical shape to go back and work in the oil fields.

When I got to Nashville I knew very few people, but there was this one guy who had played guitar with me while I was in Texas. He had moved to Nashville and gotten a gig playing with an act on the Grand Ole Opry every weekend, and he was playing clubs in the area. He gave me advice that really served me well. He said, "Whatever you do, don't spend your own money." When you're trying to make it, he explained, everyone will be coming up to you and saying that they can make you a star. They'll tell you that you need to come to their studio to cut some demos—do this, do that—and that it will only cost you fifteen thousand dollars. He said, "Don't do it. Just walk away, don't even talk to those people. If you're good enough, they'll spend their money. Just don't spend yours."

You hear a lot of other stories about people moving to Nashville doing showcases, singing demos, and knocking on everybody's door, but that's not how it happened for me. I didn't do that. I moved up there, I got a pretty good job working construction for DuPont, and I got a little house gig. There was a small club, about three miles from where I was living, and I went in and auditioned for the lady that owned the place. She gave me a job playing Fridays and Saturdays every weekend and that's all I did for awhile. Then it just started happening. I started meeting people and networking. I met songwriters and other pickers, and word started to get out. But it was by chance that I ended up meeting the president of Capitol Records at the airport baggage claim. My girlfriend, now my wife, and I were standing there and she spotted him. She knew him and we started talking and she told him, "You really ought to come out to the club and listen to Trace sing this weekend." He said okay, but I really didn't expect him to come.

Well, he showed up. I played one set and he walked up on stage, gave me his card, and said, "I'll give you a record deal." I said, "Okay." Well, that about floored me. I don't know if I slept at all that night, but the next morning I waited until what I thought was a reasonable hour and I gave him a call. I wanted to make sure he wasn't drunk the night before when he made the offer! He said he really meant it. He was signing me.

It was luck—and there's a lot of luck involved in this business. You have to have some talent, but there's a lot of luck that goes into it. But I also know that it wouldn't have happened if I hadn't taken a chance and moved to Nashville. The hard work started after I got the record deal, and it continues today. Now that I've made it this far, there are new things I want to achieve. So I just keep pressing harder.

DR. ARTHUR AGATSTON

CARDIOLOGIST AND AUTHOR OF THE
BESTSELLING *THE SOUTH BEACH DIET*

★ ★ ★

Dr. Arthur Agatston is one of the most congenial people you could meet. A few minutes after meeting me in Miami (his home), he found out that my children had accompanied me to South Beach because I had to work there on Halloween. He immediately offered me his house to use as a home base for trick-or-treating with my kids. He's that kind of guy—generous and thoughtful.

When we arrived I was shocked (but my children were delighted—they were a little leery of being at a "diet doctor's house" on Halloween) to find that Arthur's wife, Sari, had a platter full of cookies and cake laid out for them! I was pregnant with my fifth child at the time and was craving sweets, so I was happy, too! Months later, after I had the baby, I wanted to lose post-pregnancy weight and I decided to try out Dr. Agatston's South Beach Diet. I lost thirty-five pounds in five months. My husband, Mr. Hill, lost twenty-eight pounds. After dieting, The South Beach Diet Cookbook *became our guide for daily healthy eating and easy cooking. I think the world of both Arthur and Sari Agatston.*

HAVE GOALS, WORK TOWARD THOSE GOALS, AND NEVER GIVE UP

Frankly, a lot of the good advice I got early on in my life came from audio tapes. When I first became a cardiologist, I listened to tapes by people such as Earl Nightingale—self-improvement development tapes that stress having goals and working persistently toward those goals. I find that persistence is a big factor in having a successful life.

In the years when I was hospital-based and coming up with new techniques and ideas, I met a lot of classic resistance. I never gave up and I kept pushing. In fact, at our hospital we actually had the original ultrafast heart scanner called the Imatron. We used the machine for an initial study that explored whether or not qualifying calcium in the coronary arteries was a predictor of heart attacks and strokes. We lost the scanner due to economic reasons, but eventually raised money for the hospital to buy a new one. Then the hospital administration changed, and we lost that scanner again.

Still, I never gave up. I was working with Dr. Warren Janowitz, and when we completed the first paper on our findings, I was surprised that it wasn't immediately accepted by the general medical community. Many physicians felt threatened because our procedure was noninvasive and they were afraid it might replace the angiogram. It wasn't intended to do that, although it certainly was intended to prevent people from needing the angiogram. But I've realized that when you have a new idea or a new approach, you're almost always going to be faced with resistance. When I described new ideas, like the fast heart scan, to medical students or residents, they got it right away—but people who were out in practice and older were often tough to convert. Their ideas were set; they couldn't think in new directions.

PERSISTENCE IS THE KEY

It was frustrating, especially in the beginning, because I was looking for constructive criticism. I quickly became identified with the new heart scan. I developed the Agatston score, which measures coronary artery calcium, and after it began being widely used on patients I was eager to know if there was anything I could do to improve the procedure. Unfortunately, it was tough to get helpful advice or constructive criticism from my colleagues.

But then I spoke with another physician, Doug Boyd, about my frustration. Doug had figured out a better way to do a CT scan. The original CT scan moved fairly awkwardly around the body and Doug's method sped up the entire process. Even so, at first, people were resistant to his improvements. Having been through it all himself, Doug told me that new discoveries in medicine and in science often take a long, long time before they're accepted. He told me the story of Dr. Joseph Lister, a nineteenth-century surgeon who proved that using aseptic techniques decreased the infection rates and complications of surgery. Lister's discovery was revolutionary, but it took about twenty years before it was generally accepted. (And today users of Listerine have him to thank every time they gargle.) He also talked about Alexander Graham Bell, who revealed the telephone at county fairs. People used it to make a phone call from one end of the fair to the other, but they looked at it as a novelty, not as something that could be practical. Even Edison's invention of the light bulb was underrated at the time.

Dr. Boyd's stories all added up to one encouraging piece of advice: Persistence is the key.

IF YOU DON'T BEND, YOU'LL BREAK

When I first started teaching the South Beach Diet to my patients, I was convinced I had hit on something good. I'm reminded of the TV show *Davy Crockett*, which I watched when I was a little kid. "Make sure you're right," Davy would say, "then go ahead." With the South Beach Diet, I was sure I was right.

When you come up with something new, a lot of people want to take shots at you. When one school of nutrition published entirely obnoxious comments about my diet in their newsletter, my first reaction was to fire off an angry response. But I've finally learned to let those things roll off me and disappear. That comes from my mother's advice: "If you don't bend, you'll break."

GEORGE ALLEN

UNITED STATES SENATOR

★ ★ ★

Sometimes you'll meet someone new and you just can't tell exactly what kind of person he or she truly is. It's especially difficult in Washington, D.C., where folks are pretty skilled at making people like them. You don't always know where they stand.

The first time I met Senator George Allen, on the other hand, I was struck by how genuine he seemed. Working in television so long, though, I've learned that the way people appear when the camera is on can be strikingly different from how they act when the camera is off. Like most people, I knew about the senator's late father, George Allen, a football coaching legend who turned around the Los Angeles Rams and then the Washington Redskins. So I figured Senator Allen probably grew up surrounded by politicians and celebrities and had figured out how to talk a good game.

Yet each time I spoke with him, either on camera or off, he continued to impress me with how "un-Washington" he was. He is genuine, the kind of person you'd be lucky to have as your neighbor. With his easy style, he very much reminds me of one of his political heroes, Ronald Reagan.

AT LEAST THE BOMBS AREN'T FALLING

The advice that guides my life came from my parents. My mother is French-Tunisian. During World War II, the Nazis imprisoned her grandfather. When we were young, she'd tell us stories about how her family survived, but lived in constant fear. She'd recall how the Nazis would begin shooting and bombing if they saw lights. When our family faced a setback she'd always say, "Well, at least the bombs aren't falling." That led to my philosophy that so long as you stay alive, you can keep on fighting.

I grew up in a football family, and those Redskins games that my dad coached were like life or death. My father would say that losing a game was like dying—but every time you win, you are reborn. The losses would turn our house into a funeral parlor, but my mother would be there to say, "At least the bombs aren't falling." That advice always helps me keep life's setbacks or problems in perspective.

As a kid I would go astray from time to time. I considered my pranks to be good horseplay, though others did not. Dad would tell me, "You've got a great future. You have a lot of opportunities. But if you follow down this track, those opportunities won't be there. You're gonna get in trouble and that'll deny you scholarships and other things in life." I wasn't considering a career in politics then, but it got me to thinking. The advice he repeated over and over was, "Don't ruin your life by making wrong decisions."

I learned how true his words were when I was cowboying near Winnemucca, Nevada. I learned a lot about life out there. I knew I wanted to own my own land someday, and I figured the best way to learn about farming and ranching was to go out and actually work on one. This ranch was close to bankruptcy and desperate enough to hire me on. The rancher picked me up from the Husky gas station and we drove about twenty-five miles out of town. The ranch was a big one, probably around five hundred thousand acres. The days were long, hard, and hot. Most days it was me and the Cow Boss beating the cattle over the desert, up to the hills and mountains where there was some grass and water, and out on the flats where the alfalfa and oats were being grown for pellet meal. I had my own string of horses, and before sunrise I had to shoe them, water them, and feed them. After that I could feed myself. By seven in the morning, it was already scorching. It would get up over a hundred degrees. It was so hot that the only place you'd sweat was under your wristwatch. The rest would evaporate.

YOU CAN PUSH YOURSELF TO THE LIMIT AND YOU'LL STILL SURVIVE

The only conversation to be had out there was with the Cow Boss, or with the cattle themselves. The Cow Boss didn't say much, so I'd just yell general insults the cattle's way and they'd bellow back. We had 3,800 head of cattle.

Most were range cattle so you didn't have to bother with them except for roundup, but the others, close to eight hundred of them, were constantly moving. The first day I rode for about fifteen to eighteen miles. When we'd finally gotten the cattle up to where the water was, I hopped down to get a drink. But the Cow Boss said, "The cattle are already in it. It's all muddy." I said, "I've been up and going for eight hours. I need a drink." He replied, "You can go all day without drinking water." That was that. The ranch was a dot in the bottom of the valley and I was sure I'd pass out before I got back. I just prayed that my horse would follow the Cow Boss and I'd get home. I'll tell you, after the first week that saddle felt so hard it was like sitting on a spear. You'd be up before dawn and you wouldn't get back until late at night. It really taught me that you can work hard, you can push yourself to the limit, and you'll still survive.

People talk about the bickering that goes on in Washington, but it's nothing like Nevada. Whenever you had an argument with somebody about something, you literally had to fight for what you were saying. People figured that if you weren't ready to fight for what you said, you really didn't believe it. Just about everything is legal in Nevada, and you can usually get away with the things that aren't legal. Talk about the chance to make wrong decisions! When every temptation is in front of you, you learn a lot about yourself. I have nothing against people who do things that are legal in Nevada even if they aren't legal in other states, but it wasn't for me. Still, it was good exposure to the way other people lived in those days. If they got fired, they didn't care. They'd go to Seattle and hire on to work on the Alaska pipeline, the last refuge after the great western range.

IT DOESN'T MATTER IF SOMEBODY'S NOT WATCHING, BECAUSE GOD IS

While working in Nevada I was also studying to be a lawyer. On Saturday nights we would all go into town and the other cowboys would be doing things that generally got them in trouble. Because I was studying law, they expected me to know how to get them *out* of trouble. I did give them good advice, and got one guy out of a big fix. But I told them, "You can't keep doing these things. The judge won't fall for it the second time around." Some of the crimes were really serious; one time I had to talk one of the guys out of killing another. It was rough. I figure all these folks are probably dead or in prison by now. That time was one of the most formative in my life, because I was completely on my own, living by my own wits, and determining my own postulates for what was right or wrong. It was certainly hard to acclimate back to law school after that experience!

I guess what really carried me through that time was another piece of advice from my mother. She would always say, "It doesn't matter if somebody's not watching, because God is." Meaning even if you can do something that's wrong and get away with it, you never really *do* get away with it. Somehow at some point it comes back to you and everything evens up.

Carol Alt and her father

CAROL ALT

SUPERMODEL

There is a good reason models are often stereotyped as ditzes. A lot of them are. They make their living, hard work though it is, by looking good, not because they have immense intellects. Most give little thought to the inevitability of aging.

Having spent a great deal of time in the New York City area, I've often seen young girls move to town, work, shop, and party like there's no tomorrow. Often, the late nights result in late starts on shoots—to the client's dismay, and a rapid decline in job offers. Other times, young women with little experience in balancing income against expenses find themselves in debt up to their eyeballs.

Very few of them end up like supermodel Carol Alt. Yes, she is stunningly beautiful, but she is also smart. For proof, consider this: It's estimated that Carol has been on the cover of six to eight hundred magazines. She's also had sixty-five TV or film appearances, her own TV show, and her own line of cosmetics, and she's the author of a bestselling book that has nothing to do with modeling. She is a bright and refreshing role model.

SAVE YOUR MONEY

When I first started modeling, my father was very concerned about my being out in the world. We didn't know how much money I would make, or how far I would go, or how long my career would last. My father told me, "Carol, you can only sleep in one bed at a time. You can only wear one pair of shoes at a time. Save your money, because you never know what will happen." Interestingly, it was my mother who was really the saver in the family. My father spent everything. My father used to say, "We wouldn't have a pot to piss in if it weren't for your mother." That left a deep impression on me when it came to planning for the future. One day you may be feasting, the next you'll be facing famine. If you live every day like it's a feast, you won't have anything left when the famine comes. Fortunately, I was never a big spender, because when you're the daughter of a firefighter, you don't have a lot of money to go out and blow.

DON'T BE A SHOW-OFF

The first year I was modeling was a real eye-opener. I claimed the money I had earned as a model on my tax return, but didn't put down the thousand dollars I had earned babysitting. The IRS came after me, and I had to pay a big penalty. It's very hard when you start making money as a kid, especially when you haven't had a lot of money before. A lot of the models don't realize that taxes aren't taken out of their paychecks. They start making money, and they spend it as fast as it comes in. Then, at the end of the year, they have a huge tax bill and no money left.

The first time you get a windfall like that, you think about all those things you've always wanted, like a great wardrobe. I went to school with girls from wealthy families. They had great clothes, while I was wearing clothes my mother made for me. Sometimes you want to catch up on all those things you've missed and make everybody know that you're making money. But the truth of the matter is, who cares? The only person who needs to know that is you. When you spend your money to show off, you can expect the wrong kind of payback. God doesn't like people who show off.

HAVE A WORK ETHIC

When I started modeling, it was a different time in the industry. There weren't as many huge paychecks, so you needed steady work. It felt like I was working eight days a week. I was lucky, because God took care of me. Because I was constantly working, I didn't have time to spend all my money. I worked Christmas, birthdays, even vacations. I remember calling my mother from the Champs-Elysées in Paris to wish her a happy Easter. I could easily have been one of those girls who blow through all their money, if it hadn't been for my parents' advice. Instead, I saved my money.

There were also many times I could have walked away with something off the set and nobody would've cared. But I didn't, because it wasn't mine. Clients always came back to me because I had a work ethic. I didn't charge extra money each time they ran twenty minutes over schedule, and a lot of the girls did. I was grateful that they were giving me eight hours of work; I wouldn't think of charging them for twenty extra minutes. Those twenty minutes weren't going to kill me, and anyway, I probably took a thirty-minute lunch break. It amazed me how some of the other girls would nickel-and-dime the clients. Those clients came back to me over and over and over again. Ultimately, I made a lot more money than the twenty minutes over-time would have paid. I know there are a million people out there who could do the same thing I do. There are a million models just as pretty as I am, or prettier. QVC could have gone to anybody to make a skin care line, but they came to me. I think it's because they know I am willing to work hard and to put in the hours.

DON'T PROFIT AT THE EXPENSE OF OTHERS

My parents were also humble and that made a great impression on me. When I was about ten or eleven, my father and I had walked to the grocery store. We were about halfway back home, carrying heavy bags, when my father counted his change and stopped. "We have to go back," he said. I said, "Are you kidding? I'm tired." "No," he said, "we have to go back. They gave me an extra quarter." I asked, "We're going all the way back to return a *quarter?*" and he replied, "At the end of the day, when that girl is short a quarter, it's going to come out of her pocket. We shouldn't profit because she made a mistake. We should help her correct the mistake." We went all the way back and I never forgot that lesson.

PLAN FOR THE FUTURE

Because my parents were such humble people, and because I'm God-fearing, I think I view things differently from others. I'm very thankful for every-thing I have. As I've promoted my book, *Eating in the Raw,* I've been amazed when public relations people say that it's a pleasure working with me. I think, "Are you kidding me? How could anybody not be a pleasure to work with when they're trying to promote themselves?" I'll do anything I can to help them. Nothing is too little. You never know who lives where, and who might want to read what book. A little thing might be the biggest thing you ever did. Being humble and grateful allows you to notice all the great things that can come your way. Realizing that it could all change in an instant makes you plan for the future. Parents should know that it's the little examples and advice they give along the way that make a huge impression.

Denise Austin and Jack LaLanne

DENISE AUSTIN

FITNESS EXPERT

Did you ever know a girl in school who was too perfect . . . and you couldn't stand her because of it? Denise Austin is that girl—except that she's so friendly you can't help but love her!

During a conversation with her about fitness, I was complaining that I would never regain my figure after my fourth child. Denise blurted out, "Yes you can! Punch me in the stomach as hard as you're able." After a bit of deliberation, I did. It was rock-solid and flat as a board (and she has several children). I lost my argument.

That's Denise. "No" is not in her vocabulary.

THAT'S THE KEY—BE REAL

When I graduated from college with a degree in exercise, I got my first big break. I was at a President's Council dinner and saw exercise instructor Jack LaLanne from afar. I felt like I already knew him. My mother had been watching *The Jack LaLanne Show* for years and I had been following his exercises since I was a little girl. So I made a beeline for him.

I introduced myself, explained that I had some really great aerobics exercises, and asked if he'd give me the chance to come on his show to demonstrate them. It was 1981, and aerobics was just starting to catch on in a big way in America. Jack told me he'd love to have me on, so I called him the next Monday. The very next morning I was a guest on his show. I got along so well with Jack and his wife, Elaine, that he asked me to become his cohost. I'd never had a show before, and I asked Jack what was the key to his success for all these years. Jack told me, "Just be yourself and people will love you. That's the key—be real."

So Jack gave me great advice *and* my big break in television. I just love him so much. It was the turning point in my life, because until then I really thought I was going to be teaching physical education or corporate exercise programs. Instead, my life changed from that moment on. Jack is still one of my greatest friends and I speak with him all the time. He's ninety years old, totally fit, and a wonderful mentor. Jack not only works out daily, he still works! I'd love to be like that when I hit ninety.

SMILE AT PEOPLE

My mom, who passed away recently, was my ultimate role model. I have two daughters, and one of the most important things my mom told me was, "Let them be who they are." She did that for me and I'm doing that for my kids. Everyone is different and everyone possesses unique and special qualities. As a parent, you have to help bring out the best in your children. That doesn't mean that you have to push them in a certain direction, or that you should leave your kids to fend for themselves. Rather, just try to help them to find out what makes them happy. My mom was always there for me, but she never pushed me. It's amazing—she had five kids to take care of, yet she was always there to give us a boost. She had a positive outlook on life and she would always say to me, "Smile at people and someone will smile back. It doesn't cost you anything and you get something in return."

I was a gymnast from early on and was always doing flips around the house. I'd do tumbles off the coffee table, or move the furniture so that I could practice my routines—and my mother always accepted it with a laugh! So I let my kids do things like that, too. I encourage them to play. One of my daughters is very spirited and the other is a little more artsy and creative. I relish their differences. My oldest is now a great lacrosse player and wants to play in college. I'm supporting her but not pushing her. I want her to be well-rounded and balanced, while also maintaining her passion for the sport.

I graduated from high school in 1975, the first year women were offered scholarships in sports because of Title IX. I was offered scholarships from twenty-one different colleges. Some of them were major universities, but my mother never told me which one she preferred for me to attend. She let me choose the one that felt right to me.

THE HARDER YOU WORK,
THE LUCKIER YOU GET

Probably one of my best qualities is that I believe in myself. I truly believe I can motivate people and get them off the couch. I never take no for an answer. I have an incredible amount of determination and perseverance. In 1984, I tried twenty-eight times to get Steve Friedman, the executive producer of the *Today* show, on the phone. No one had ever done fitness on the program. I called and called, without success. Then, on the twenty-ninth call, I got him on the phone and told him that America needed exercise. I promised that I could show people how to make their stomach flat and how to exercise in the workplace. Steve agreed to let me come on the show, and that led to a job there for four straight years.

I learned about hard work from my father. He was on the St. Louis Browns in 1946 and '47. He's in the hall of fame at Loyola University in California for baseball. He always exposed us to different types of sporting events and I really looked up to him. He always said to me, "The harder you work, the luckier you get." People always tell me, "Gosh, you're so lucky you have your own TV show, exercise tapes, and products." I respond, "Yeah, but I work hard for it." Nothing comes easy.

GOOD SHAPE = GOOD SELF-ESTEEM

I honestly believe that if you're in good shape, good things fall into place. If you feel better about yourself, you'll have better self-esteem and more confidence. Being in good shape is a wonderful way to empower women and help them realize that they can do more in their life. Just the sense of accomplishment after a workout helps women. You can overcome depression and many other problems through exercise. You see that in kids, too. If they're in sports or some form of activity, they feel better about themselves and have higher self-esteem—especially teenage girls.

I work out only thirty minutes each day. I wedge it in, often before my kids wake up, so it doesn't take away from my time with them. I start the day off right, and it just doesn't take that much to get in shape. You just do something for yourself—like take a walk for thirty minutes every day. Our family has always been very active. My mom was the New York state jump-roping champion when she was sixteen years old. We laugh about it now, but she found a way to have fun, stay fit, and accomplish a goal. When we were little kids, my mom would put on music and dance with us. I do that with my girls now. Just have fun with your kids—that itself leads to great exercise and great times.

Tiki Barber and his mother

TIKI BARBER

PROFESSIONAL FOOTBALL PLAYER

★ ★ ★

A leading league rusher at five feet ten and two hundred pounds, Tiki Barber of the New York Giants defies the odds. He knows that. But they are the odds other people set for him. Tiki is doing exactly what he wants to do, and that is being his best. He's wanted that his entire life.

Tiki, though, is much more than what any of us see on the football field every Sunday. He is one of my two favorite people to host a television show with (and the other one is in this book, too!). He is intelligent, kind, thoroughly professional in all that he does—a man who gives back to others in a million ways. Along with his twin brother, Ronde, he published the book By My Brother's Side, *which is based on their childhood. It teaches young people about the values of family and hard work. Both brothers work to promote literacy; together they founded the Barber Brothers' Literacy Champion website. Tiki is a board member for the New York City Children's Miracle Network and the Fresh Air Fund; he frequently visits families at the Ronald McDonald House of New York City, is involved in Citymeals-on-Wheels, and was awarded the Humanitarian Award by the United Hospital Fund's New Leadership Group. It would be a waste of time to list his pro football records, because he is sure to set new ones next season.*

When I think of people who truly deserve the success they have, Tiki is at the top of the list.

BE PROUD AND PLAY PROUD

When I was young, my mother gave me the best piece of advice, although I didn't understand it at the time. She always told me, "Be proud and play proud." She meant that it was important to fight against adversity—and to believe in yourself, so that other people will believe in you, too.

My mother raised my brother and me on her own. Sometimes she worked several jobs, so we gained our independence early. But we tried to stay out of trouble, because we wanted to make sure she was proud of us. Her advice taught us how to be good students and good athletes.

SCHOOL BEFORE SPORTS

Mom didn't just tell us how to behave; she was also a wonderful example for us to follow. When Ronde and I went to college, she went back to graduate school to get her master's degree in business administration. Our education was always the top priority. When I was growing up, we could never go play sports unless we had our homework done. You would always see Ronde and me on the bus ride home, scrambling to finish our homework so our mom would be proud of us and then we could go out and play sports.

Then, when we all went off to college, she would call us every week. She'd say, "I'm getting straight A's. What are you getting?" It was peer pressure, even though she wasn't our peer. Only when we got older did we realize that she'd found a way to motivate us. It's easy to be a good athlete if you have athletic skill, but it's hard to do the other things right—and she found a way to motivate us to excel both on and off the field.

NEVER GIVE UP ON YOURSELF

At age forty-three, my mother was diagnosed with breast cancer. She's a survivor, and she said, "I'm not going to die." She handled it phenomenally. She was so strong that it made it easy for us to handle it. We wanted to return home and help her, but she said, "No, your schoolwork is important. I can get through this and I'll be fine." In fact, she had surgery on a Sunday and we had a game that next Saturday. She made it to the doctor's that day for a checkup and back in time for the game. It's that kind of "I'm never going to give up on myself, so other people won't give up on me" attitude that I admire and try to have in my own life.

GIVE OF YOURSELF TO YOUR CHILDREN

My mother's father died in Vietnam, but he'd been very strong and independent even while growing up in such turbulent times. He found a release, I guess you could say, in the military, although it forced my mom's family to move a lot. They moved not only around the country, but also around the world. That experience shaped her, because she was exposed to different cultures and different ways of doing things. As we got older, her experience trickled down to us.

My mom is a person who has to feel challenged. When Ronde and I first got drafted we said to Mom, "You should rest. You should quit your job," because after the first six months in the NFL we realized we could take care of her. We said, "You need to relax and let us take care of you because you've worked so hard for us for the past eighteen years to make sure we never wanted or needed anything." She really did work her backside off to take care of us. Well, she did leave her job for about five months. Then she told us, "Boys, I'm bored." So she went back to work for the County of Roanoke as a budget administrator. That is how she's always been. She's never asked anything from us. She's given everything and we really owe her.

GET RIGHT OUT THERE PLAYING

I know how hard it is to grow up in a single-parent household. My mom had to go to every game. She had to be the disciplinarian when we got out of line, bringing out the belt and putting us over her knee. She took on the roles of both mother and father. One time, when we were about fourteen years old, there was even a big football game where the parents played. It wasn't flag football or powder puff. It was real football with pads and helmets. Our mom was right out there playing, and she immediately gained our permanent respect. I could never say no to her after that.

BE BETTER THAN ANYONE ELSE IN ACADEMICS

A lot of times, kids get caught up in their parents' dreams. Their fathers or mothers want their children to be athletes and they lose sight of what's really important. I think our mother really understood this because my father was a great athlete at Virginia Tech. He had the chance to play in the pro ranks, but he got caught up in the negative part of the game and it ruined him and it ruined their marriage. For a long time, it ruined our family. So Mom knew that your education is really what it's all about. You can be walking down the steps one day and break your ankle and it's all over. I know my career is getting on, and eventually I'll have to do something else for the next fifty years of my life. I need an appreciable skill and my mom realized that. She made it a challenge for us. She'd say, "Okay, you're good at football. But be good in academics. Be better than anybody else in the class." As a direct result of this advice, everything we did became a challenge.

YOUR FAMILY WILL BE THERE FOR YOU FOREVER

My mother always emphasized to me that family was the most important thing in life, and that my brother was someone who would be there for me forever. It was always put that way. It's funny, because Ronde and I would always fight, but then we'd go to the playground together, and no matter how mad I was at him, if some kid picked a fight with him I'd immediately defend my brother. If you went after one Barber brother, you'd end up fighting two. I think it's how we'll always be.

FIND WHAT MOTIVATES YOU

A lot of those things Mom did for us—the lessons she taught us, the hardships she went through—we didn't know about until we left the house and were on our own. Then, we started to understand her sacrifices and it made us appreciate her even more. She literally devoted eighteen years of her life to us. She didn't have a boyfriend. Everything she did was for us, and that's an enormous sacrifice for a twentysomething-year-old woman. You know, other kids who didn't have a mother like ours didn't often develop the same kind of drive. A lot of them didn't have to work; they weren't forced to work.

You don't have to be poor to find that drive, though. Take the example of John Lynch. He used to play with my brother; he's a phenomenal human being. Most people in the NFL—and I'm not trying to stereotype—are determined to work hard so that they can escape poverty or the old neighborhood or a bad situation at home. But not John Lynch: he grew up with a silver spoon in his mouth. But he has drive, and at age thirty-two he's just as strong a player as he was twelve years ago. John teaches me that everyone has to find his own unique motivator that will help push him toward success.

CRITICS ARE YOUR FRIENDS; THEY SHOW YOU YOUR FAULTS

I think what motivates me is proving people wrong. I grew up in an area where people made assumptions about me based on the color of my skin. Later, people said I couldn't succeed on the college level because I was too small, but then I did. They said the same thing about me in the NFL—even if I got in, they said, I'd only be used as a third-down situation kind of guy. But eight years later, I'm the all-time leading rusher in Giants history. Those little jabs motivated me.

Critics are not your enemies. They're friends who are willing to show you your faults. That's how I view it. When I know things are going bad, I look to see what people are saying about me, and then I learn what to change and improve.

James "J. B." Brown, number 41, DeMatha Catholic High S...

JAMES "J. B." BROW

SPORTSCASTER

★ ★ ★

Several years back, J. B. Brown was scheduled to fill in as my cohost on Fox and Friends. *When I mentioned it to my husband, he said he thought J. B. looked familiar, and that they might have played basketball against each other in college.*

Well, since J. B. hosts Fox NFL Sunday, *I was sure he'd played football. I asked J. B. about it the next day, and to my surprise, I learned that he'd played on Harvard's basketball team. Furthermore, he remembered Mr. Hill for an effective (but not entirely legal) move he made on the court during one of the Penn-Harvard games. Since then, J. B.'s been a frequent guest on the show. While I am always so impressed by his vast knowledge of history and current affairs, he is widely recognized for his TV sports commentary, first on CBS Sports and then with Fox. J. B. has hosted three Super Bowls, two Olympics, the NBA finals, ten years of the NCAA tournaments, and NHL pregame shows. Among his numerous awards are Sportscaster of the Year from the American Sportscaster Association and two Emmys for Outstanding Studio Host.*

So his resume is impressive. But anyone who has had the good fortune to spend time with J. B. will tell you something far more impressive: that he is simply one of the finest human beings one could meet.

EARN THE RIGHT

The foundation of my life was most actively, aggressively, and consistently set and reinforced by my mother and father. My father was absolutely in the picture. He worked as a prison guard, drove a taxi, and worked at an Avis rental agency. Sometimes he held down all three jobs at once. He worked hard so that my mother could stay home and raise five kids, of whom I'm the oldest. My mom would keep us in check, but she also always encouraged us to grow. She knew just the right words for whatever situation or challenge we were going through. My mom has a high school education, but my family says that she has a Ph.D. in common sense. She always helped me understand, even when I started to show some athletic talent, that I had to *earn the right* to participate in sports, by making certain that I was being the best possible student. Academics always came first in our house.

ACADEMICS COME FIRST

I'll never forget when I was recruited by the local Catholic high school, which was a powerhouse in sports as well as an excellent academic institution. I went there and earned a position on the varsity team as a freshman, even though I didn't get much playing time. Even as a freshman, I had reached the apex: This was the school everyone wanted to attend, and here I was on the varsity team.

Then, one day, something atypical happened. The coach kept us a little later than usual. Well, my mom called up to the school to ask where I was because I wasn't home at the appointed hour to be at the kitchen table—which was our study—doing my homework. The assistant coach who answered the phone said, "Mrs. Brown, he's out on the basketball court with the rest of the team." She said, "You don't seem to understand. He's due home within the hour to be doing his homework, and if he's not here then consider him off the team, because his schoolwork comes first." The head coach agreed. That underscored the emphasis my mom placed on academic excellence: She knew it was the key to success in life, and she made sure we knew it too.

TRY TO DEFUSE STEREOTYPES

Former senator Bill Bradley was a big hero of mine because of the success he enjoyed as both a basketball player and a student. I vowed to myself that, if I could get into a great school, I would go there to try and defuse the stereotype that African American ballplayers thought about sports first and academics second. I thought it would send such a wonderfully positive message to my peers. I decided to go to Harvard University. Things did not work out for my teams, but I would absolutely make the same decision today. I chose a school like Harvard because Bill Bradley inspired me to find success both on and off the playing field.

WHEN YOU POINT YOUR FINGER TO BLAME, THERE ARE THREE FINGERS POINTING BACK AT YOU

Probably the seminal moment for me in terms of the game of life was when I was picked by the Atlanta Hawks in 1973 during the fourth round of the NBA draft. (This was during the time when there were two professional leagues, the ABA and the NBA.) I went to Atlanta, and the coach told me he only had one spot available. But I had confidence, and I thought I could make the team. Pete Maravich, a great basketball player on the Hawks, told me, "Wow, you can really play! Just keep on working hard, and things will work out."

About a week later, after a hard practice, I was in the whirlpool and the coach sent for me. I thought he must have been summoning me to his office to congratulate me on how well I was doing. Instead, he told me he was cutting me from the team. I said, "Coach, you've got to be kidding!" He replied, "You've got a great education and things will work out for you." I explained, "That's not the point. I want *this* team to work out for me. Why are you cutting me?" He didn't have a really good answer. I thought I was a better player than the guy he chose. I flew home, crying all the way, and hid in the house for about two weeks. I was afraid to show my face because I was so embarrassed.

But you know what? When I looked in the mirror, I realized I couldn't answer this one question that my high school coach Morgan Wooten, who's in the Basketball Hall of Fame as one of the greatest high school coaches ever, had always asked us. He would say, "In the off-season, when some guys sit around lollygagging, someone else is out there working hard to perfect his craft and hone his skills. If those two people were to ever meet on the basketball floor in competition, who do you think would win?" I thought about how hard I had worked in high school. Then I asked myself: Did I have the same strong work ethic in college, or had I wasted time, acting like the big man on campus? It turned out it was the latter. I didn't work as hard. So when I looked at myself in the mirror, I could not truthfully say that I had worked as hard to stay on top as I had to get to the top. Again, I heard my mother's voice ringing in my ears. She'd say, "Before you start looking to place the blame elsewhere, remember that when you point your finger to blame someone else, there are three fingers pointing back at you. So look at yourself first."

After the Hawks cut me, I made the commitment to myself that I would never ever let an opportunity pass me by because I was ill prepared. That's why I get teased sometimes about doing so much, because I've had that driving passion ever since. I'm blessed in being the cohost of *Fox NFL Sunday;* I host a nationally syndicated radio program on sporting news radio; I'm one of the correspondents on HBO's *Real Sports with Bryant Gumbel;* I host HBO's pay-per-view boxing coverage, splitting duties with Bob Costas; and I host *America's Black Forum,* a kind of syndicated *Meet the Press* focusing on African American issues. Howie Long teases me by asking if I have Jamaican blood because I work nine jobs! But all of that is an outgrowth of my commitment to work as hard as I can.

ABILITY IS YOUR JOB SECURITY

In my twenties, I worked within corporate America, first for Xerox and then for Eastman Kodak in their sales and sales management departments. I thought I was on a pretty great career path, aiming to become a corporate executive, maybe even a division president. Then I started moonlighting as a broadcaster for the Washington Bullets, who are now called the Washington Wizards, and the media bug bit me. I remember asking a lot of people in the business for advice and input about what the broadcasting industry was like. Most people told me that the environment was tenuous, because there's no real job security—unlike, say, government work.

I remember talking to Mike Trainer, the attorney for the boxer Sugar Ray Leonard. I spoke with him about my job dilemma. At the age of twenty-eight, I was looking to broaden my horizons and move into broadcasting full time. I was concerned about leaving a stable job and the growing success that

I built through hard work at Xerox. I asked him if he thought I'd be able to get my sales job back if broadcasting didn't work out. He said, "You have a scholarship mentality. You want a guarantee that you will have a safety net. The game of life doesn't work that way." Then he said, "Son, the only security you have in this world is in your ability to perform well. If you can do the job well, it makes no difference what the environment is." That fired me up. I told him, "You're right. I'm going to go for it, because I'm passionate and I think I'm good enough and hungry enough." Thank God it has worked out.

GOD PUTTETH DOWN ONE
AND SETTETH UP ANOTHER

We're a family of faith. My mother raised us in the church. I'm a firm believer that no matter what the situation is, God will always make room for your talent. Boy, did I have to hold onto that belief when I wasn't able to realize my dream of playing professional basketball—and again later at CBS. After I'd been there for a number of years, I was looked at as one of the new breed of guys being considered for A-level broadcasting assignments, possibly even the voice of a major sport or lead studio host. But then CBS lost football broadcasting rights to Fox, and when new management took over at CBS Sports, I wasn't tapped to be one of the two or three leading announcers. I was crushed; I cried like a baby. It was very painful. I had to take comfort from the belief that God would make room for my talent. I relied on Psalm 75, which essentially says that promotion cometh neither from the east, nor the west, nor the south. But God is the judge. He putteth down one and setteth up another. So I had to wait, and indeed an opportunity presented itself at Fox. I've now been blessed to be the cohost of the number one pregame show for eleven years running.

GET EQUAL FOOTING

Recently, I spoke to a group of children at an elementary school in a depressed section of Washington, D.C. It was their career day program and teachers were rewarding academic excellence. Several children got to read their essays about their career aspirations. Quite a few of them wrote about how they wanted to be professional athletes because of how much money they would make, the influence they would have, and the way people would respect them. In a way, it hurt me a bit, because I wanted to drive home the point that academic excellence is the foundation. But I could understand some of their hopes and desires, because so many youngsters in challenging environments are being raised by kids themselves. They see sports as their ticket out of a bad situation. They're constantly bombarded with images and messages of athletes being the ultimate symbols of success.

When I see parents getting so excited about their kids' athletic abilities, I wonder if they're as excited and passionate about their children's academic pursuits. I often think back to something that my mother always told me: "Someone else may be naturally more intelligent than you, but they're given no more time in a day than you are to accomplish something. They may have more talent, but if you have more passion, study harder, and 'lock in your knowledge,' you'll be on equal footing." Quite frankly, I can work with brilliant people and not feel intimidated because I know I can work hard.

President George W. Bush and E. D. Hill, 2004

GEORGE W. BUSH

43RD PRESIDENT OF THE UNITED STATES

★ ★ ★

Those who know the president well say that the most influential advice his father, former president George H. W. Bush, ever gave him had nothing to do with politics. The respect that the president has for his father is well documented, as is his father's unconditional love for his son. According to friends of the family, it was his father's shrewd advice that set Greorge W. on his course to the presidency. Despite stereotypes that imply that the president is not smart or curious, friends say that he is constantly broadening his horizons. Those who spend a great deal of time with him away from the spotlight report that he's an avid reader and a remarkable listener. It is said that one of the best things about working for him is that he respects the advice he receives. He may not always agree with it, but they say he never belittles anyone. His style combines several of his father's mantras: Be humble, don't think you already know everything there is to know, and stay alert for that next opportunity.

BROADEN YOUR HORIZONS

Early in 1973, I had a discussion with my father. I had been out of undergraduate school at Yale for about five years, and was contemplating my next move in life. At the time I was considering going to business school at Harvard, but I wanted my dad's opinion. My dad told me to seize the opportunity to continue learning. He said, "This is a perfect opportunity to broaden your horizons." I can still hear him saying that phrase—"broaden your horizons"—to this day.

USE YOUR TRAINING

As a result, I went to Harvard Business School, where I not only learned about business, I also gained a new level of confidence to embark upon a business career. As you know, I am the first president ever to hold an MBA, and I try to use what I learned there to keep my administration disciplined and results-oriented. My father's advice taught me to push my boundaries and to never stop learning.

DEAN CAIN

ACTOR

★ ★ ★

Quite a few television and movie actors come through the Fox studios, and when they do the staff members can be counted on to drift in and meet their favorites. Still, I wasn't quite prepared for the reaction when Dean Cain arrived. Every single summer intern, and the vast majority of females in the newsroom, found an excuse to come by the greenroom!

They weren't disappointed. These women actually swooned! To start with, Dean Cain is an intelligent man, with a history degree from Princeton University, where he also was captain of the volleyball team and an NCAA record holder on the football team. After college Dean was signed as a free agent with the Buffalo Bills, but when a knee injury ended that career he turned to acting. Soon he became Superman in the television hit Lois and Clark: The New Adventures of Superman. *Not just a pretty face, Dean is a smart businessman who prefers to control his own destiny. He started his own production company, Angry Dragon Entertainment, which produces the syndicated series* Ripley's Believe It or Not!, *in which Dean now stars while he continues his movie work.*

IT'S NOT PERSONAL

The best advice I've ever gotten came from my father. He told me, "It's not personal." That's an important sentiment that I pass on to other actors. As an actor you're always trying out for various roles, and when you don't make the cut it's easy to take the rejection personally. But you have to remember that the casting people don't know you, so their rejection really has nothing to do with you personally.

Unfortunately, a lot of actors don't see it that way, and they become dejected when they don't get a role. I found that when I stopped taking rejection personally, I started getting more parts. It gives you a different attitude.

Along those same lines, I once read a great bit of advice from Richard Drey-fuss. He said that each time he doesn't get a role, he tells himself that the people who didn't hire him were idiots! I've adopted that philosophy. If I want a role and don't get it, I fully believe they're idiots, and that they made a huge mistake!

IF YOU BELIEVE THE GOOD PRESS, YOU HAVE TO BELIEVE THE BAD

My dad also taught me not to believe my own press. A lot of people say that, but then they don't follow the advice. The problem is that, if you start be-lieving any of the good things written about you, you have to believe the bad things as well.

PERSEVERANCE MAKES THE DIFFERENCE

When I played for the Buffalo Bills, I learned an important lesson. It was ac-tually written inside the standard issue Bills playbook that we got when we arrived at training camp. It said something like, "There is nothing as com-mon as a talented man who is unsuccessful. Perseverance makes the differ-ence. Those who persevere will succeed." That has always resonated tremendously with me. I truly believe that those who push really hard, and continue to believe in what they're doing, are the ones who will succeed.

ALWAYS BELIEVE YOU WILL WIN

When I was in high school, along with football, I ran hurdles. My father told me, "Your greatest strength is your optimism. Never lose it." One time I was lined up against an incredibly fast and strong opponent. Dad said that he knew I believed that either the other guy would slip, or I'd get a great start, or the wind would blow in the right direction. *Something* would happen, and I would win even against a better hurdler. He was right. And from that day on, I learned to be optimistic and to start every race with confidence.

I'LL BE DADDY. YOU BE CHRISTOPHER

My greatest inspiration is my son, Christopher. He is so pure and wonderful and filled with love. To watch this child grow, and hear the things he says, is amazing. Honestly, the greatest piece of advice I've received came from him. He says, "I'll be Daddy. You be Christopher." Then he imitates me. What I learned from watching him impersonate me is incredible. The way he speaks to the dogs makes me think, "Oh my gosh, that's the way I talk to them." Sometimes he acts rough and tough, and it makes me look more closely at how I act in front of him. Watching him play Daddy makes me a better parent.

Dr. and Mrs. James S. C. Chao with their eldest daughter, United States Secretary of Labor Elaine L. Chao (right), *and their youngest daughter, Angela Chao* (left)

ELAINE L. CHAO

SECRETARY OF LABOR

★ ★ ★

What happens to a woman who has attended Mount Holyoke College, Harvard Business School, MIT, Dartmouth College, and Columbia University and has twenty honorary doctoral degrees from colleges and universities across the country? She becomes the secretary of labor!

Elaine Chao is much more than your average well-educated woman. She was the director of the Peace Corps, expanding its presence into newly independent countries. Following a financial mismanagement embarrassment, the United Way of America hired her on as president and she restored trust to the organization. Upon her appointment to his cabinet, President George W. Bush described her as a person with "strong executive talent, compassion, and a commitment to helping people build better lives." She exemplifies what it is like to live the American Dream.

WE WERE GOING TO MAKE IT
BECAUSE WE HAD HOPE

A lot of different people encouraged me in my lifetime, believed in me, and inspired me. Being an immigrant is one of the seminal experiences of my life. First and foremost, my parents are incredibly inspiring. The civil war that marked the first half of twentieth-century China was the era in which my parents grew up. As teenagers, they were both on the refugee trail, fleeing first the war and then the Japanese who were invading China. All they wanted in their young lives was to find stability and peace. In 1949, they moved and resettled in Taiwan. There, they met, got married, and started our family.

One of their dreams was to find economic opportunity and freedom for themselves and for us. My father grew up in a rural village devastated by the civil war, but he was smart, adventurous, and very entrepreneurial. After he arrived in Taiwan, he took a national examination and earned the highest score. In fact, he broke all the records! Because of that, the government sponsored him for further study in the United States. It was a tremendous honor. So he came to America alone, not speaking the language very well and leaving behind his wife and three young children. It was a very, very difficult adjustment for him. His father, my grandfather, died while my father was in America; he had not been able to communicate with his father since he left China. But my father continued to pursue his dream.

After three long years, my father was able to bring the rest of us to America.

I entered third grade without understanding a word of English. I copied whatever was on the blackboard into my notebook, and every night after my father returned from one of his three jobs he would go over the notebook with me. We would review that day's lesson, and that's how I learned English. It was hard for him sometimes to decipher my childish scribbles. And because I didn't understand the alphabet, I would sometimes flip the Bs and Ds and Ps and Qs, so it was even more confusing. But those long nights of studying and reviewing my notebooks forged a deep bond between father and daughter. I cherish that as one of the great blessings of my life.

The difficulties were different for my mother. She didn't speak English. She stayed at home to take care of the three children. We lived in a small, one-bedroom apartment in New York City, and every day her husband, who was her lifeline to the outside world, would leave to go to work. She was petrified that something might happen to him and that he wouldn't return home at night. Because she didn't speak the language and wasn't working, she lived in daily fear that if he didn't come back she wouldn't know what to do. She didn't have anyone to call. She didn't know about nonprofit organizations, community groups, and the network of social services that could . help. Her fear was so deep-seated that it wasn't until some forty-two years after she arrived that she told all of us about it. About two Christmases ago, my mother finally let loose and revealed how frightened she was when she first came to America. My sisters and I were amazed, because growing up, we were enveloped in the love our parents had for us, and we didn't really recognize how difficult or challenging life was for our family. I just knew that on field trips my classmates would have lots of money and be able to buy all sorts of souvenirs and other things that we couldn't afford. All I had was a few extra pennies to buy the milk for lunch. There was no money for extras. To this day, I can still remember hearing the jingle of the Mister Softee ice cream truck as it wound its way through the neighborhood. Usually, we didn't have any money to buy ice cream. But each month, after saving all we could, we would have enough money to buy one ice cream treat for the three of us. We would be so excited! We would wait for the ice cream truck, negotiate amongst ourselves, and finally select one ice cream to share among us. To this day, that is the best ice cream I've ever tasted.

My parents' optimism shielded us a great deal, because they were absolutely confident that we would have a better tomorrow, that life was going to get better soon, and that the adversities we faced would be surmountable. We were able to make it because we had hope. We were convinced that, ultimately, we were going to get to a better place. We felt we were so blessed already because we had been reunited as a family.

My parents were a very brave young couple, and their story and our story are common within the immigrant community. That's why I understand how difficult it is for immigrants to come into this country and into this society. I think the most valuable piece of advice that I ever received was to never give up. It came from my father, who said, "Nobody can defeat you but yourself."

Throughout all the difficulties in my life, I've tried to remember his words whenever I needed encouragement. I keep a little picture of my grandfather's native village in China, which I visited in 1981 when China opened up. In the picture, there are thatched huts. There are chickens and pigs running around in the dirt. When I see that picture, I think: If my ancestors could survive in an environment like this and do well, then surely I have a little bit of their grit and I can survive anything.

My family's experience affirms the tremendous opportunities that are available in this country. Opportunity is there for those who are willing to work hard and to follow their dreams. I was the first Asian Pacific American to assume leadership positions in all three sectors of society: public, private, and nonprofit. When I entered the federal government in the Reagan administration, it was very rare for Asian Pacific Americans to work in government. When I was appointed president and chief executive officer of United Way of America, there were very few Asian Pacific nonprofit leaders. I'm the first Asian Pacific American woman to be appointed to a president's cabinet.

DON'T BE A VICTIM

Reflecting upon where I've come from, and how far I've come, helps me to keep things in perspective. I know that there are real challenges and difficulties in life. Other people can be unfair or unjust, but I have never let that deter me. I basically forged ahead with confidence in the Lord, and with the support and love of my family. I knew that in America if I made the best of my abilities, planned ahead, and worked hard, I would be okay. My father's adage about not defeating yourself was very useful. I try to pass it along to young people, telling them, "Don't be a victim!" Sometimes there will be unfair treatment, and there will be discrimination. And where there is discrimination, we must fight it! But it's also important to be honest with oneself and distinguish discrimination from personal shortcomings. Each person is responsible for knowing his or her own shortcomings and working to overcome them.

I told my parents how much their love and counsel meant to me when I became secretary of labor. I was very grateful that my parents were able to attend that swearing-in ceremony in the Oval Office with the president. Like many immigrants, they devoted their whole lives to improving the lives of their children. They sacrificed a great deal by coming to this country without the comfort of family or close friends, because they wanted to access better economic opportunities and freedom for us. We've come a long way since those days. But I've never forgotten what it is like to be a newcomer or an outsider. I'm a better leader today because I understand that and I have empathy for those who are new to our society. I want to empower them. I don't want to add to their burdens by giving them false expectations, or weaken their chances of success with advice that will not strengthen them. This is a great country, and if they believe in themselves and don't give up, most of the time the results will be quite positive. Newcomers need to understand that, because the only thing worse than discrimination is to compound it by accepting the low expectations that come with it. We all must realize that our future is up to us.

Senator Norm Coleman and his wife, actress Laurie Coleman

NORM COLEMAN
UNITED STATES SENATOR

★ ★ ★

You can learn everything you need to know about people by going out fishing with them. Are the fish they catch really as big as they claim? Do they get mad when the fish aren't biting? Do they appreciate the beauty of nature? Do they blame the lure, the wind, other fishermen, or anything else for an unproductive trip? And, most important, do they offer to bring bait and snacks?

As you may have guessed, Mr. Hill and I have gone fishing with Senator Norm Coleman and his family on a number of occasions. It takes guts for a senator from one of the great fishing states to go fishing with a TV reporter. He's bound to know that what happens on the water doesn't necessarily stay on the water! Our first fishing trip several years ago was a bust. Eight hours into the trip, I'd caught a few scrawny fry. Then the senator felt something on his line. It turned out to be a clam! (For those who don't know . . . that's not the way you're supposed to catch clams.)

When we headed back in to the dock, though, from the way Senator Coleman acted, you'd have thought it was one of the best fishing days ever. That's just the way it's supposed to be. Catching fish is great, but the stillness of the water, the beauty of the pine trees, and the time to enjoy it all is equally important. Senator Coleman gets it.

ALL CRISES PASS

When I was mayor of St. Paul, I had a sign on my desk that said "All Crises Pass." I didn't have it there for myself. It was for the numerous people who came to my office. When you're the mayor, people come in and tell you how the sky is falling. They may have been talking about a political problem or a personal problem, but no matter what, it was always the *worst* thing in the world. Well, I knew it wasn't the worst thing in the world, because I know what the worst thing is. [Senator Coleman's first son, Adam, was born in

1983 and lived for six weeks. His daughter, Grace, was born in 1992 and lived for three months. He has two other children.] When you've gone through great tragedy, everything else is relative.

In my political life, I lost an election to Jesse Ventura. According to my pollsters, Jesse didn't even figure into the race. The night before the election they told me that my only real competition was the state attorney general, and they said I was beating him by up to seven points. Instead, I lost to Jesse. I went back to work the next morning.

Later in my career, I ran against Paul Wellstone in an election for the senate seat he that held. On Friday, December 27, 2002, Paul and I both attended an election rally in northern Minnesota. Later that day I got word that Paul's plane had crashed, and that he, his wife, and their daughter had died. Upon hearing the tragic news, my family and I immediately went back home to St. Paul. On our plane people were praying; my wife was in tears. It was an overwhelming tragedy.

Back in St. Paul, my campaign staff was talking about what to do next. I said, "We have to shut things down. Take all the advertisements off the air. Everyone needs to take a breath and pray for the Wellstone family." My mom and dad and my sisters were there at my house because they had flown in for the election. A group of reporters came to the door and wanted a statement. My staff told me, "Don't say anything. Don't issue a statement." I got on the phone with my campaign managers, and they were all saying the same thing: "Don't issue a statement, because anything you say could be turned against you." But my wife walked up and said, "We're going to go outside and show what's in our heart." So I'm walking toward the door with the phone to my ear and on the phone they keep saying, "You can't go out there." Finally, I said, "I appreciate all the good advice, but I'm going out." So we walked out the door and had a conversation with the media. In the end, I think that race was about showing your heart. I think, particularly after that great tragedy, people were looking more at our heart than anything else. Certainly all the political gurus were averse to risk. But I think the pivotal point in the whole race was when my wife said, "Show your heart."

In the next few days, there were all these political questions resulting from Paul's death, questions about what I was going to do now that Walter

Mondale was replacing Paul on the ballot. I remember talking to reporters and telling them, "Look, this is just an election." Yes, it was an important election, but it was also a time to grieve and to step back and reflect on what happened. It was a time for more important things. I know what the most important thing is, because in life I've experienced the worst thing in the world. I've learned I can handle everything else.

Well, after I ignored their advice, all the politicos left me alone. It liberated me. That moment fundamentally changed my life. If I'd reacted differently, I don't think I would be a senator. When I reflect on why I'm here, it reaffirms my belief that every time a door shuts another door opens: every time. Because I know that all crises will pass, I'm not as knocked down by adversity.

I GOT HERE BECAUSE ONE DOOR WAS SHUT AND ANOTHER DOOR OPENED

I always work as hard as I can, but I also accept the outcome of things. I don't know if it's a sense of faith or just a sound belief that God opens doors, but I've seen that in my life. I got here because one door was shut and another door opened.

In 1993, as a Democrat, I was elected mayor of St. Paul, even though the party had endorsed someone else. My party was in one place, and I was in another. I wanted to merge units of government, I wanted school choice, and I had a different position on abortion. Basically, they wanted the status quo and I wanted change.

At the beginning of my first campaign, I made a commitment to run for two terms. In my second race for reelection, I decided to run as a Republican. At that point everyone thought I would lose, because St. Paul is a city that is overwhelmingly Democrat. However, I decided to take a chance. In the end, it was about going with my heart. Years later, during my Senate race, the commercial everyone says won the race for me featured my daughter sitting on the steps of our house. She talked about how I never stopped working until I accomplished what I set out to do. At the end of the commercial she said, "I just want you to know that my dad has a good heart."

I truly believe that these races are about heart. I think that's why President Bush won his second term. People saw the heart of him. You always have to remember that some people are going to hate you whatever you do, and some people are going to love you no matter what you do, but the folks who decide your fate will be able to figure out what's real.

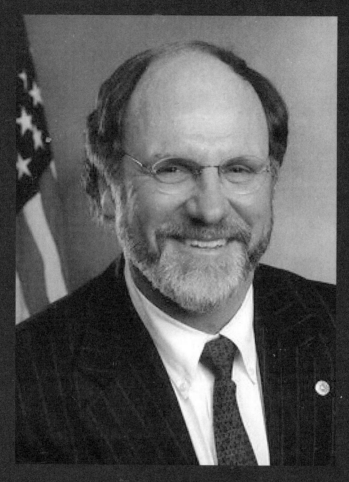

JON CORZINE
UNITED STATES SENATOR

★ ★ ★

Jon Corzine is well known for making the leap from being a powerful CEO of Goldman Sachs, with no experience in public politics, to becoming a U.S. Senator. Although he is labeled a liberal Democrat, he made his large fortune by wisely managing money and a huge, profitable corporation. He knows how to save a buck and where to spend one. His business record speaks for itself. When the national dialogue focuses on how businesses can grow while struggling with ever increasing health care costs and foreign competition, he understands. He's been there. He knows that unnecessary programs will sink a firm or a country. He's competed against companies overseas. While Senator Corzine firmly tows his party line, I find that when it comes to money matters he will give a very honest answer to a very direct question. His experience before going into politics means he can help propel our nation toward a more prosperous future.

MAKE YOUR OWN CURIOSITY

I grew up on a farm in central Illinois. My parents' lives were framed by a good Methodist upbringing. My mother was a schoolteacher; my father farmed soybeans and corn and sold insurance on the side. I worked right alongside him on the farm, like most other kids in our area. Child labor standards were ignored by farmers like my dad. Consequently, early in life we learned the value of a good day's work. In that era, you weren't swamped with television and movies and lots of stimulation. You had to make your own curiosity or fulfill it by reading and educational experiences. I had very powerful instincts about learning, and I had a very competitive, can-do attitude.

BEAUTY IS AS BEAUTY DOES

Like most individuals, my life was shaped by my parents. They focused on making sure that I was educated and that I enjoyed learning. They were also competitive as heck! My folks were pretty strong disciplinarians, but I never viewed learning as an ordeal because they taught me how to make it fun. In addition, if I came home with a B or a C on something, all hell broke loose in my house. Because of that, I tended to be quite diligent in my studies, and that work ethic carried over into sports and everything else that I did. My parents taught me to do things well just because that's how things should be done. My dad had a line that he'd use when I came home to show him my grades: "Beauty is as beauty does." He meant that the grade was secondary to the knowledge I gained while earning it. Each time I would try to say that a grade or a score was good enough, he'd stop me and say, "It's not just what is good, it's how you do it. It's not good enough just to win."

THINK ABOUT LIFE IN DIFFERENT CONTEXTS

In Taylorville, Illinois, I had a couple of teachers who set high expectations for me. Taylorville is a small town, and not many people who lived there when I was growing up had a cosmopolitan view of the world. A French teacher changed my view. My teacher, Darryl Merriman, signed up a bunch of fifth-graders to take French. Our group began to learn the language, and decided we wanted to go to France after our sophomore year in high school. There were fifteen of us in that fifth-grade program, but it was pared down to about six of us in the end. We had bake sales and held car washes to raise money for the trip. It was the first time I'd ever been on an airplane. Once I got to France, my future was changed forever. I loved visiting a different country, experiencing another culture, and after I returned I set high expectations for my life going forward. Mr. Merriman taught me that to think about life in a different context is a very powerful thing.

COMMONALITY

There was a gee-whiz element that developed early in my life. Walking down the Champs-Elysées, I was thinking to myself, "I can't believe I'm here." I wished I could see more and more new places. No group from our school ever recreated that exchange program. We ended up thinking we were special. We felt we had a tremendously unique experience, and we did. At least for me, it laid the groundwork for doing something other than coming back to my hometown and settling there for my life. I was curious about what was going on in the rest of the world.

That first trip to Paris formed the person that I'd become later in life. In politics, it allows me to understand that there are lots of different perspectives on how you get to common goals. It taught me to find the commonality we share. People's lives generally revolve around their kids and families. While there may be different cultural aspects, deep down most of us value the same things.

SERVE YOUR COUNTRY

My father was a World War II veteran and I grew up in the Vietnam era. I think all of us from that era, in one way or another, examined whether we were going to participate or head out. While I grew unsupportive of the war as it continued, I was very clear that I wanted to be responsible in the context of American military service. When I got the chance to join the Marine Corps, I took it. If you want to really know what you're made of, go through training with the Marines. Their rigorous standards taught me discipline and physical stamina. Though I realize that there's a big difference between being a reservist who, by fortune, doesn't get called up and one who was actually in the crosshairs.

COMPETITION IS A STIMULANT

There is no question that competition is a stimulant that motivates me. I was always involved in sports. I was captain of the basketball team. I think that competitiveness led me to Wall Street and, later, to politics. What I've accomplished in politics, or what I did on Wall Street as a trader and in leading Goldman Sachs, in competition against Morgan Stanley or others, has all played a part in shaping who I am. But I can't forget the little lessons I learned on the streets of Paris, or at the dinner table with my parents. These, too, are part of who I am.

JOHN DANFORTH

FORMER UNITED STATES SENATOR

★ ★ ★

I don't know whether to call him Senator John Danforth, Ambassador Danforth, or Saint Jack. He's a bit of each. What is most noticeable about him is that regardless of whether you ask a Democrat or a Republican, you'll hear the same thing: John Danforth is honorable, admirable, and honest. He's been the attorney general of Missouri, a U.S. senator, and a special envoy to Sudan. He left government in 2005 after serving as the U.S. ambassador to the United Nations. An ordained Episcopal priest, he officiated at the funeral services of top Republicans and Democrats alike, including Katharine Graham, who owned the Washington Post, *and former president Ronald Reagan.*

Most remarkably, when you ask him a question, he doesn't tell you what you want to hear; he tells you what he thinks.

I DARE YOU

My grandfather, William H. Danforth, was the founder of Ralston Purina Company. He was a charismatic person before charisma became such a widely used word. He was also a very formidable man. He wrote a book that sums up the advice that changed my life: It was entitled *I Dare You.* One of his expressions was "Inspire nobly, adventure daringly, and serve humbly." But his basic message to me was "I dare you"—meaning that he dared me to have big aspirations. Not so much to serve myself, but to serve others. It gave me a sense of commitment. I had to take risks on behalf of the kind of life in service I aspired to lead.

As a result, I don't think I would ever have been satisfied leading a boring life, or one where my main goal was finding out how much money I could make. There was always a sense of obligation, that I should be doing more and making the most of my life. Another one of his slogans was "My own self at my very best all the time." That was the kind of person he was. He was eighty-five years old when he died and to the end he was a very dynamic person and particularly interested in inspiring young people.

I was interested in politics from a very young age. Politics isn't just about public service—it is also about energy and taking the kinds of risks and dares that appealed to me. My grandfather's personality, style, and vigor changed me and inspired me. They showed me that I had an obligation to do something with my life.

DO WHAT FEELS RIGHT

Another person who inspired me was Robert Rankin. By now I've lost contact with him, but if he's alive today, he's close to ninety years old. He was a Methodist minister and vice president of the Danforth Foundation, which was founded by my grandfather. When I was in college, I intended to go to law school and then run for political office, but between my junior and senior years I realized that I wanted to go to divinity school. I wasn't really sure whether I had a calling or not, but I felt compelled to go. But when I got to divinity school, I soon realized that it was not what I should do with my life. There were two possible outcomes: working in a parish, or teaching religion. I did not think I had the temperament to be a parish minister. I now know I certainly didn't! I wondered whether I had an obligation to become a minister, or whether I should go to law school. I didn't know what to do.

I really respected Bob Rankin, so I asked him for his opinion. He told me that there wasn't an obligation if it wasn't right for me. He made me realize that I had to go with my gut, and continue hunting for a position that really felt right for me.

FOLLOW YOUR INSTINCTS

So I went on to law school, but I kept taking courses at divinity school. Since I wasn't going to work in a parish, the question became what I should do with that degree. George Cadigan was the Episcopal Bishop of Missouri. Should I become ordained? I had a lot of conversations with Bishop Cadigan on the subject, hoping he would tell me what to do. He wouldn't. Instead, he just kept asking me questions. At one meeting, over Christmas vacation during my last year of law school and divinity school, he asked me, "Jack, what do you want to do?" I said, "I think I should be ordained." And he replied, "Then you should." It was the right choice. I've always practiced law and politics and never worked full time in the parish ministry, but it's always been in my life. There is no doubt that it is a large part of who I am. It's a piece of my makeup.

Interestingly, George told me later that the standing committee of the diocese absolutely did not want me to be ordained. They knew I intended to make law or politics my career.

PUSH FOR SOMETHING BIGGER

After law school, I went to New York to practice for three years; then I moved back to Missouri. Wayne Millsap was a lawyer and a very creative political thinker in St. Louis. I hadn't known Wayne, but he called and asked if he could come over and introduce himself. He believed I should run for public office—and that it should be a big office. At first, he thought I should run for Congress, but then concluded that I should run for state attorney general. He was strong in his beliefs and persuasive.

I was thirty-two at the time of the election. I was really young and green. I had only come back to Missouri in 1966 and this was 1968. In a way, Wayne Millsap was like my grandfather because he wanted me to take the daring step. He was always pushing me to run for something bigger. When I was thirty-four, I ran for the U.S. Senate against Stuart Symington and lost. It wasn't until 1976 that I won the Senate seat. Wayne was a grab-the-brass-ring type of a guy. By nature, I'm a go-for-it type of guy because of influences like his.

FOLLOW YOUR NOSE

Bob Teeter was the founder of Market Opinion Research, a polling company. He was also a really good human being. He was very perceptive and smart and had very distilled advice. I'd been elected to the Senate, and I was about to leave for Washington when I called Bob and asked if he had any advice. He said, "Yes. Follow your nose." That has stuck with me ever since. It is just absolutely great advice. In other words, trust your instincts. Make decisions based on what seems right. I have passed that on to so many people, particularly young people, who are interested in politics. If you have to sit down with a big, long legal pad and draw lines and columns, you're never going to do it. It is all about instinct.

Donna (far left) *with her sister, Joanna, and her father, David, 1963*

DONNA DE VARONA

OLYMPIC SWIMMER, SPORTSCASTER,
AND FOUNDER OF THE
WOMEN'S SPORTS FOUNDATION

When I see Donna de Varona, it's usually as a blur. She's following her kids, rushing to Washington, D.C., for another meeting, or working on a new project. She's been on the go almost since she was born. At age thirteen, Donna was the youngest member ever to join a U.S. Olympic swim team. By seventeen, she was bringing home Olympic gold in both the four hundred meter medley and the four hundred freestyle. She was voted "Outstanding Female Athlete" in 1964 by the AP and UPI. After setting eighteen world records, Donna used her winning personality to open the door for women in all sports. Any woman who played on a college sports team owes her a debt of thanks.

A WAY OF LIFE, NOT A HOBBY

I loved playing sports as a young girl and watched my brother play on a lot of teams. Back then, girls didn't have the same choices. There were very few options. I really wanted to play Little League baseball, but only boys were allowed to join. The only position open to me was "bat girl." It was that experience that would later inspire me to be very involved in crafting Title IX, which opened up girls' sports.

Since baseball clearly wasn't my future, I discovered swimming. I won my first meet at age nine, and by the time I was ten all I wanted to do was be in the pool. My father understood an athlete's dedication. He'd been an All-American football player at the University of California and a Hall of Fame rower. When I told him my heart was in swimming, he told me, "It's a way of life, not a hobby." He gave me a six-month trial and told me I had to make every practice, with no excuses. That meant I'd have to give up things like birthday parties and trips if they conflicted with my practice times. If I wanted to succeed in sports, practicing and competing would be my life. It turned out that I was ready to give up all those things. That realization set me on my path for the Olympics.

BALANCE THINGS OUT

Dad was right; I missed a lot of parties. But my mom helped balance things out. She insisted that I go to the big dances and let me run for class officer. But all of that was in addition to my training. The result was that I graduated from high school as a pretty normal kid. I led fund-raisers, was a class officer, went to my brother's football games, and still swam up to six hours a day. I'm not sure if today many kids would choose that kind of life. We didn't have the distractions they do. There were no DVDs, PSPs, or nonstop television channels. It really was better to go to a swim meet on the weekend than to hang out at home.

FIND NEW BARRIERS TO BREAK

I wonder just what would have happened to me if I hadn't been able to put my energies into the pool. Fortunately, I was successful at swimming from the start. I made my first Olympics at thirteen. Then, in the 1964 Olympics, I won two gold medals. I think my parents were really proud of me. My father understood the journey and knew how to prepare me. He was my first coach and was a great one. He just got it. He was naturally open to finding better ways to train. Later, when I realized that I needed to work with a different coach and learn new techniques if I were going to make progress, he understood.

When I set off for college at UCLA there were no women's athletic programs. So I stopped swimming. Then in 1965 I broke a new barrier, becoming the first female broadcaster on ABC's *Wide World of Sports*. By 1972 NBC had hired me to cover the Olympics, and I reported for ABC during the 1976 and 1984 Olympic Games. The sports experience, coupled with my work on television, led to an opportunity that changed the direction of my life.

BE INVOLVED IN PRESERVING
YOUR FREEDOMS

I served on President Ford's Commission on Olympic Sports. That led to Senator Ted Stevens asking me to work in the Senate. I was at a fund-raiser in New York and Ethel Kennedy happened to be attending. I asked Ethel what she thought I should do. She said, "You should work in the Senate, but don't work for any specific senator. Work for a committee; you'll be able to bridge the political divide that way." I followed her advice and went to work in Washington in 1976 as a special consultant to the Senate. That led to working on the Amateur Sports Act of 1978, which reorganized Olympic and amateur sports. I've been working in Washington ever since, on Title IX and other issues. The Olympic and sports movement is bipartisan, and Ethel's advice gave me more flexibility while I was working on the Hill. It also changed my life by making me more interested in the political process. It made me realize that we all have to be involved if we want to preserve our freedoms.

MAKE SURE SACRIFICES PAY BACK DIVIDENDS

Following my father's early advice gave me an edge. Every time I worked out, I'd work to exhaustion. In my television work I could do it all—write, report, and even produce. Dad said, "If you're going to do something, do it 100 percent; you don't want to make the sacrifice and not have it pay back dividends." I think I had that determination within me, but we all need mentors. I marvel at the kids who succeed in sports without fully engaged parents, because it's a tough journey. There are all kinds of hurdles and barriers, whether it's winning, or becoming a target for everyone after you start winning, or going through the changes of a young adolescent girl wanting to be competitive but also more feminine. The support of my family really made a difference.

LET YOUR PARENTS KNOW HOW IMPORTANT THEY ARE

I wrote both my parents letters at the end of their lives and told them how important they were in my development. I think every child should do that. Because once they're gone, if you've never expressed what they meant to you, you'll regret it.

BASH DIBRA

PET BEHAVIORIST

★ ★ ★

In terms of sheer passion for his profession, it would be hard to top Bash Dibra. His love for animals, especially dogs, is written all over his face. When you meet Bash, you are immediately overwhelmed by his huge smile. This is a man who enjoys what he does. But there's more: He has passionately committed his life to improving the lives of animals. He is the bestselling author of several books, including the most recent Star Pets, *and is the creator of Pet Therapy Week.*

SOMETIMES VICIOUSNESS IS ONLY A ROLE

In 1953, my parents and I escaped from Albania and got caught in Yugoslavia. We were thrown into a camp. To make sure you didn't escape, they had attack dogs patrolling the camp. I grew up in that environment, from the age of two until I was nine.

What really helped me keep my sanity, and inspired me, was my experience with the killer dogs. Our family had been pretty wealthy, although we lost all of that when we fled. We had always owned pets. When these attack dogs confronted me, my parents told me, "Sometimes a pet that shows viciousness is not really vicious. It just has to play its role." With that understanding, I started looking at the dogs and thinking, "Wow, maybe they're really not mean." Evil forces certainly existed in this camp, but the animals were a positive force.

What my parents tried to teach me was that not everyone is mean. They wanted me to know that kind people do exist, despite the cruelty that we witnessed at the camp. The same went for the animals. Not every dog is mean; they just have to play a role. After gaining that new perspective, I closely watched the dogs and came to believe that they could be friendly.

Sadly, the guards used the dogs to torture people. They had little games:

They would tell the prisoners that whoever ran faster than a dog through a certain field, and jumped over a fence, would get extra food. Of course it was a lie: They wanted people to run to help them train the dogs to be more vicious. Eventually, the dogs were programmed to attack if people ran. Think of *The Manchurian Candidate,* when someone was programmed to respond as if to the push of a button. That's how the dogs acted. Humans are always in control of animals, but in our situation, humans were using the animals to control other humans.

As I watched the dogs, though, I began to see them in a whole different light. Gradually, I started sticking my hand through the fence—without letting any of the guards see me because it was against the rules. Little by little, these killer dogs began to trust me and would come and lick my hands. Something wonderful just developed from there. We had a secret kind of life. I would always go and talk to the pets. They would touch me, and I would touch them and hug them through the fence. We didn't have much food in this horrible setting, but I always brought a morsel of food to try to befriend them more. Surprisingly, the dogs became the catalyst of my freedom.

ALWAYS GIVE BACK

Then, one day, the guards caught me. They couldn't believe the dogs loved me so much. It fascinated them that these killer dogs could love a little boy. They took me behind the wall so no one could see what I was doing. What they didn't realize was that I would mimic the guards when they were training the dogs. I would say the same things they were saying to the dogs. They watched me command these savage dogs, and were amazed that they would listen to me. That was the start of an unbelievable journey in my life.

Those attack dogs were really pet therapy for me. Befriending them inspired me to work in the world of animals. We all are equal to our pets, but what makes us human is that we can learn about love and caring from animals. They actually make us better people. Even the guards were forced to be human with me, since it pulled them out of their power position because the dogs listened to me as much as they did to them. A lot of privileges came out of this. The dogs made my life at the camp better, and I promised myself that I would always give back to the animals.

SEE THE GLASS HALF FULL

After we were freed from the camp, we traveled all over Europe. I was still a child, and it was fun, especially in Rome, to go to those *Cinema Paradiso*–type movie houses. I'd go into a room and watch a picture being shown on a wall. There, as a child, I remember seeing the old Charlie Chaplin movie *A Dog's Life*. Charlie saves the dog from a pack, and the two become friends and partners in stealing food. I loved watching the animals, and realized I wanted to train animals that worked in films.

After I got to the United States in 1964, I became a pet behaviorist. I had the chance to work with Rudd Weatherwax, who was Lassie's trainer, and Frank Inn, who was Benji's original trainer. Later, I had the opportunity to raise a timber wolf named Mariah. I raised her from a pup until she was about fifteen. She was my Rosetta Stone. She taught me how to understand the world of animals. She taught me how they act, how they behave, how they live in society, and more.

Who knew then that a horrible experience in a government camp would lead to my life's work? Destiny created the path. For that I am grateful, and I'm optimistic for the future. I always try to see the glass half full.

STEVE DOOCY

TELEVISION HOST AND WEATHERCASTER

★ ★ ★

What needs to be said? Steve is the entertaining and talented host and (frequently inaccurate) weatherman on Fox and Friends.

THERE'S ALWAYS A WAY TO DO SOMETHING. IT'S OUR JOB TO FIGURE OUT WHICH WAY.

I grew up in rural Kansas, the son of Depression-era parents. We didn't have much, and I spent a lot of my childhood watching my parents walk around turning out the lights behind us. As a kid, I dreamed of one day having a new car like the other families, or having a nice house with water you could drink right out of the tap. (Our home had well water that was high in toxins and low in quality. It was okay to wash with, but scary to drink. So we carried water from Abilene to our kitchen for twenty years.)

College seemed like something my parents would not be able to allow me to attend. But my father, Jim Doocy, told me that anything was possible. "There's always a way to do something," he said. "It's our job to figure out which way." And with that I started my lifelong method of approaching a problem, analyzing it completely, and then solving it. I figured how to get to college without costing my parents a dime. It cost me almost every waking minute, because I wound up working three jobs at once to pay for everything.

When I started in television, one of my first bosses offered up the key to successful broadcasting. "If you don't throw up in the first thirty seconds, you'll be fine." Twenty-five years later, I'm still fine—100 percent puke free.

Perhaps because I come from humble roots, I have never been comfortable spending money on myself. When I buy my wife a car, I get her the safest, most luxurious ride on the road. But when it's my turn, I'll get myself a stripped-down vanilla car, with no bells or whistles. I hate to waste resources on myself; I'd always prefer to spend them on my family.

DELAY GRATIFICATION

In *The Road Less Traveled,* M. Scott Peck begins with a summation that has resonated for many of us. He writes, "Life is hard."

And it is.

He also writes that it's better to delay gratification as long as you can, before you treat yourself. So many today just want "the good stuff"; they don't want to be bothered by the humdrum, the routine. They want to take the Express Lane to Easy Street. I was taught that Easy Street is your end goal. The meal won't be satisfying if you start with dessert. *Delay gratification:* I try to get my kids to understand that idea, but because their parents are giving them the things they didn't have growing up in the 1960s, there isn't much delaying of anything. Every day is gratifying. And that has bothered me. But what my wife, Kathy, has taught me is that what really matters is the quality of life. And she's absolutely right. Why should I delay my personal gratification until the end of the road, when I'm wearing black socks and short pants at my gated community in Boca Raton? Still, how lousy would it be to wait your whole life for something, and then find out that it never happens? Your car brakes fail; you eat some bad shellfish; you fall down the stairs headfirst. After all, I may never make it to Florida! So I better live a life worth living now.

Sure, I still turn out the lights behind my kids. I marvel at how I can drink the water right out of the tap at home. But I don't delay the good stuff in life. I look for it every day. In my kids, in my wife, in my friends, in my work, and in myself.

As my father said, "There's always a way to do something. It's our job to figure out which way."

This is my way.

Emme and her mother, Sally, 1968

EMME

MODEL

I figure that anyone secure enough to go by her first name alone must be pretty impressive. And WOW . . . is Emme impressive!

First of all, she's stunningly gorgeous. She's been selected by People *twice as one of their 50 Most Beautiful People, and* Glamour *selected her Woman of the Year. She's also a Revlon spokesperson. On top of that, she is an incredible businesswoman.*

Emme was the first full-figured supermodel. Many would be content with that achievement; not Emme. She's also been the host of Fashion Emergency *on* E! *Entertainment Television and the Style Network, a bestselling author, a wife and mother, and the creative director of her own clothing line, developed exclusively for women sizes 12–24. Further, she is the chair ambassador of the National Eating Disorders Association (NEDA). And she was the first model to speak about these issues before a congressional subcommittee.*

RELY ON YOURSELF TO GET WHAT YOU WANT

When I was very, very young, I remember my mom working two jobs. She was divorced, but by working hard she was able to provide a nice home for us. Her father had been very wealthy at one time, and whenever we would go and visit him she would say to me, "This is not yours. This is just what you were born into. Never look for someone else outside of yourself to get what you want." She was anxious for me to understand this, because she had a difficult relationship with my grandfather. For whatever reason, he hadn't stepped in to help her when she was a struggling single mom. She learned that she couldn't rely on him for help. But when we visited him she wasn't bitter or angry. She just loved him for what he was and left it at that. She never moped or griped. She never let me see her that way.

My mother died when I was still pretty young, and when my grandfather passed away I wasn't expecting anything, so I wasn't disappointed. I enjoyed my relationship with him, and thank goodness I didn't set myself up by thinking I wasn't going to have to work.

BRING IT ON

Watching my mother work several jobs taught me to develop a very strong work ethic. I always wondered why my mom had worked so hard when other moms were home with their kids, but I was never upset or bitter over it. It was just a matter of fact. At fourteen, I got my first job fixing divots on a Durham, North Carolina, golf course. There's nothing like your first paycheck, because you can say to yourself, "Now I have a little bit of freedom." Throughout high school, I had a few jobs during the summers. I worked at a Sonic Drive-In. I babysat. I never shied away from work. I always thought, "Bring it on."

FIND YOUR PASSION

I have always tried to appreciate opportunity. I went to Syracuse University on a full sports scholarship and majored in speech communications. I never thought I was going to get into modeling—no way, José. You must be kidding! I knew I was going to be involved in television, and I wanted to work in sports broadcasting.

After college, I immediately flew out to L.A. I was lucky enough to get a job as a page at NBC, and learned the business from the bottom up. I took as many production assistant jobs as I could get, just to gain the experience. On the job, I gravitated toward the camera and the human interest stories; these interests led me to news reporting. I took a job in Flagstaff, Arizona, where I had no friends or family. I quickly learned, to my deep, deep disappointment, that hard news wasn't something I was going to enjoy. Although the stories motivated me, I wasn't the type who heard about a disaster and thought, "That's going to look good on my audition reel." I knew early in my career that I was passionate about people, but I wasn't sure I wanted to be a reporter.

Yet my friends all told me that if I stopped working in television, I'd never get back in. They said it would ruin my career.

GIVE OPPORTUNITIES A TRY

While I was in Arizona, I'd heard about full-figure modeling. Some people had even contacted me, encouraging me to try it, but I just dismissed it. I moved back East, to New York City, and got two jobs: one at an investment firm and another selling real estate. Then, one day, I was reading an in-flight magazine when I noticed an entire article on full-figure modeling. I started laughing because two days before that I'd been on the phone with someone who was urging me to give it a try. I fit the bill: five foot eleven, size twelve to fourteen, attractive features. I thought, "You know, I've always pushed this away. Maybe I should give it a try."

So I decided to go knock on the door and see what they had to say. My boss was great; he let me try out for the modeling jobs on my lunch hour, as long as my work was done. I started landing jobs internationally, and while I was overseas I ended up finding more new business for the real estate firm than I did when I was in the office. But it was clear that the big money for me was in modeling.

At a certain point, my accountant said to me, "You've got to pee or get off the pot. You can't do too many things at once, because you won't do well in any of them. You have to focus." That was very good advice: Jack-of-all-trades but master of none isn't the way to get to the top. So I focused on modeling, and soon I started getting booked by the top modeling clients. And it wasn't long before I realized how important it was to have a representative of women of all shapes and sizes.

LOOK AT WHAT IT WILL TAKE
TO FULFILL YOUR GOALS

It sounds crazy, but while I'd been working in real estate and at the investment firm, I'd also started Emme Associates. I had gotten my massage certificate, and I was planning to open a massage business in the World Trade

Center with two sets of therapists. I was going to relax Wall Street! I'd even had business cards printed up. But then I became so passionate about what I was able to do with modeling that I put that aside and focused on my true career.

I always wish I had nine lives; I have so many impulses and thoughts and ideas and visions and I'd love to pursue them all! What I've learned to do after I get an idea is to look at the ten steps it'll take to achieve, and decide if it's really what I want. I'm a proven example that you can do a lot by determining what it is you want to accomplish and then focusing on it.

DON'T TRY TO DO IT ALL YOURSELF

Of course, there can be a downside to being so driven, determined, and self-reliant. Giving up control, for instance, isn't easy for me. I realize now that I can work with others and end up with a better product, but it's hard to learn that. It is very difficult for me to hand off responsibility, because I'm so focused on being self-sufficient.

Back in 1993, I remember, I was trying to pay all my bills while traveling 150 days a year. I did that for three years in a row before I finally hired an assistant. It was even tough for me to allow someone to clean my house, because I just felt I should be spending every weekend cleaning. I was so focused on being a good housekeeper, being a good wife, being a smart businesswoman, that it was tough to admit I couldn't do it all. I finally realized that at the end of the day I needed to be me and not drive myself crazy. I had to step back and ask my husband, "Can you take care of the car oil changes?" and "Can you take care of the recyclable stuff in the garbage?" There's always going to be that little voice inside my head telling me that I should do it myself. But you only have so much energy; sometimes you have to admit you need help.

The first meeting of Sarah Ferguson (far left) *and Prince Andrew* (back to camera), *1971*

SARAH FERGUSON

THE DUCHESS OF YORK

★ ★ ★

We Americans may not want a monarchy here, but we're always intrigued by what's happening in the British royal family. The world first encountered Sarah Ferguson when she married Prince Andrew and became the Duchess of York. She was part of a fairy tale world we peeked into. And we watched with the same fascination as the fairy tale collided with modern problems. During her divorce Sarah was vilified by many of her own countrymen and found refuge in America.

In appreciation, she's giving back. Most people don't know about her work for American charities, including Chances for Children, an organization she established in 1994 to help needy children in the United States. The charity provides everything from HIV testing for at-risk children to school supplies for students in poor districts.

DON'T LIVE INSIDE YOUR HEAD

When I was twelve, my parents divorced and my mother abandoned me in Argentina. From that moment on, I felt worthless. I believed that somehow I had broken up their marriage, that I had ruined the entire family. When my mother left, I turned to food for comfort. It became my life. There was nothing else. Food was my way of feeling loved and cared for. It was my way of ignoring the pain of losing my mother. My father worked seven days a week, and when my sister went to live in Australia, I felt as if I'd lost my entire family. The housekeeper brought me up.

At the age of twenty-five, I married a prince. While I may have looked and acted like an adult, I still felt like the little lost girl from my childhood. I was totally illogical and focused on myself. Because I was living inside my head so much, I didn't realize the ramifications of any of my actions. People who didn't know me well thought I had it all—to them, I was a confident and bright girl leading a glamorous life. But it was all a complete lie. Andrew was the only person who really understood me. When we got married, it was with real love. He is my best friend in the world because he was able to fall in love with the real Sarah, the twelve-year-old without all the facades. Even though I didn't open up to him, he was able to see me for who I was. And when I looked at Andrew I saw a sweet young boy.

We'd met for the first time when I was about twelve and I think that's when we fell in love. This is the first time I've tried to describe it in these terms. When you're a prince, you have to put on a different aura in front of the public, to keep the mystical value of the monarchy. But we met before we had all that weight on us. Our love is the same as it has always been. We see each other for our true selves. We're so happy and content together because when I married my prince, I was also marrying my best friend. That's why our daughters are so happy and why they're so strong and confident. Andrew and I don't have to be married to maintain the wonderful love that we forged at such a young age.

THE CHOICE BETWEEN LIGHT AND DARK

Most of my life I have lived with FEAR—by which I mean "False Evidence Appearing Real." I have a powerful imagination that sometimes makes me think the worst. I've been so driven by fear all my life that darkness has often been my identity. In the past, if you told me fifty times that I looked pretty or that I was a good person, I would have categorically denied that you were right. That's just how my mind would process things.

What I eventually learned, however, is that there's a choice we all make in life between light and dark. I didn't realize that until four years ago, when I met a psychoanalyst named Anamika. She is the only person who has ever challenged me to really examine how I react to other people. I'm constantly telling her, "You just don't understand royal life. You don't know what my life is really like. I'm really a horrible person. You don't have to deal with the press." Luckily, she's strong enough to stay on the line and tell me, "No, Sarah, you're wrong."

At first I challenged her fiercely and was horrible to her, because I was sure she would eventually leave me like others had. But she wouldn't. Instead, she started helping me dismantle my sanctuary of darkness. There was some light coming through already, but still I was afraid to relinquish that dark place where I oddly felt most comfortable. Most people would have told me not to be so rude, but she said, "I'm not getting off the telephone, and we're going to work through this." She'd ask me questions like, "Isn't it true, Sarah, that all your life you have believed that you weren't a good person?" And I'd respond, "Well, yeah. But that's true. That's how I am." She would say, "Yes, you've believed this about yourself. But it's not true. What about . . ." and she'd bring up some good thing I'd done.

Two months ago, I received a letter that told me what a wretched person I am. I called Anamika and read her the letter, which said, "I have never met a person as horrid as you. You make people feel small." Anamika asked me, "Well, is there any possibility that you've been a bit strange with her? Or a bit quick? Have you noticed that you can do that sometimes?" And I acknowledged that was true. She said, "Write her and say you're sorry and ask forgiveness for your behavior." So I wrote her a letter and cleaned my side of the street.

I feel lucky to have met someone like Anamika. She has made me realize that we all have the ability to find peace within ourselves and with others.

GO IN SEARCH OF YOUR SOUL

I'm driven to become a better person now and to know God. I don't want to have a car or house. That doesn't interest me. I don't want any form of materialism. I simply want to do His will. So I went in search of my soul.

On a trip to India, I took a train from Delhi to Dar es Salaam to have an audience with his Holiness the Dalai Lama. He epitomizes compassion through humor and utter contentment. I thought maybe he would be able to help me learn to live with the regret I felt. So I sat there with the Dalai Lama and he asked me, "So why are you here?" And I said, "Because I have to ask you: How do you live with regret?" He responded, "Regret? Have you made so many mistakes?" And I said, "Yes, I have." And he said, "No, actually you haven't." And I said, "Well, I have." And I proceeded to list all the things I've done wrong and regretted. He stopped me and said, "But you are a good mother." I said, "Well, yes, I think I am a . . ." But before I could get the words out, he repeated, "Good, good mother." And I firmly said, "A good mother, yes." He replied, "Well, there is nothing better." And he slapped his hands together the way monks do.

Then he said, "You mention the word 'guilt.'" I said, "Yes, I feel so guilty, because I've hurt so many people. I didn't think about the ramifications of my actions." And he said, "No, I don't know what 'guilt' is, because it is not a word in Tibet. It is not in our dictionary, because guilt is not real. What you feel is your own fabrication; it is not real. So you move on and you don't make the same mistake again." So I said, "Yes, I guess." Then he said, "Okay, you go." And as I was leaving he said, "You clear?" And I replied, "Yes." But he said, "No, you're from England. It rains every day there, so it's not daylight for you yet." Meaning, I wasn't totally clear yet, but if I kept being a good mother and a good person, I would continue down the road toward self-contentment.

Geraldine Ferraro and her mother, Antonetta, 1948

GERALDINE FERRARO

POLITICIAN AND PHILANTHROPIST

I recall the first time I saw Geraldine Ferraro. She took the stage in St. Paul, Minnesota, as Walter Mondale announced her selection to be his vice presidential running mate on the 1984 Democratic ticket. Regardless of your political bent, it was a thrilling moment for women, young and old. My generation was the first that really had every option open to them. But to see this—a woman on a presidential ticket—made it sink in.

Later, Ferraro sponsored the Women's Economic Equity Act, which ended pension discrimination against women and enabled stay-at-home moms to open IRAs. Honestly, I never fully appreciated what women like Ferraro and others featured in this book had gone through to bring women to where we are. To hear that any company would overlook you for a job simply because you were a woman now seems ridiculously antiquated, yet it was a real concern for her generation.

Today, Ferraro is the executive vice president of HF Global Consulting Group. She works with several philanthropic organizations, including the Antonetta Ferraro Scholarship Fund (named for her mother) at Marymount Manhattan College, and the Multiple Myeloma Research Foundation, which researches the disease she was diagnosed with in 1998.

GET UP AND MOVE ON

My father died when I was eight years old. As a kid, you look at the world and wonder how you're going to be able to handle a loss like that. It was very difficult for my mother, too. She was the most adoring and loving woman. She explained to me, "Life will give you some tough times. What you've got to do is get up and move on. If there's anything you can do to make it right, do it. If there's nothing to be done about it, then move on."

My mother was very smart. When she graduated from eighth grade, the principal of her school told her that she should go to secretarial school. But her family wouldn't let her go to high school, because she had to go to work to help support the family. All of her life, I think, my mother felt that if she'd had an education her life would have been different. She was determined to provide her own children with a great education. I've got to tell you she had to struggle, but she did it: ours was second to none. I went to Marymount Manhattan College on a scholarship—something I would never have been able to do otherwise. Then I went to Fordham Law School at night. I got the best education the city could offer, and I know my mother was proud. In fact, I'm not sure if she was more proud when I got the vice presidential nomination or when I graduated from college.

FIND A NEW CHALLENGE

I will always cherish my mother's advice about the importance of knowing when and how to move on. When I get tired of doing something, I go and find a new challenge. Even when I've run into hardships in my life, I try to keep moving.

I look at my life and it's strange, in a way—I've held so many different jobs. And that's in my adulthood, not counting my job as a replacement secretary or even my five years of teaching in the New York City public school system. When I graduated from law school and tried to get a job at a law firm, they told me, "We aren't hiring women this year." Companies could get away with discrimination back then. Some days, I'd go through five or six interviews and hear the same line. When I give my speeches now, I always tell the story about the first firm that turned me away. In the past, I didn't name names. But now I do, and it's so much fun, because inevitably there are a number of women partners in those firms now, and they stand up and applaud.

Once I had my children, I stayed home for thirteen years. When I went back to work full time, I worked as a prosecutor and assistant DA in Queens County. During my four and a half years in the DA's office, I was a bureau chief; I created a Special Victims Bureau—a precursor of the "Special Victims Unit" you now see on television. When I couldn't find any new challenges in the bureau, I looked for something new. So I ran for Congress, won, and stayed there for six years. I think if I hadn't gotten the Democratic nomination for vice president, I probably would have run for Senate in 1986 against Al D'Amato. After the 1984 campaign, I became a managing partner for the New York office of a national law firm. Now I'm the head of a global public affairs office in a consulting firm.

Fortunately, my mother lived until 1990, so she saw my success in several fields. She saw the 1984 campaign. In fact, I think she was the only one who really thought we had a chance to win! She was so proud.

In some ways, it was good that I wasn't in the White House, because I got to spend much more time with her. As she got older, I was able to take one day a week off to be with her; we'd spend hours in the park, having lunch or just talking. I loved those afternoons; they were the kind of times you can't replace.

Steve Forbes with his father, Malcolm S. Forbes, and his daughter, Elizabeth, 1989

STEVE FORBES

EDITOR IN CHIEF, *FORBES* MAGAZINE; PRESIDENT, FORBES INC.

Steve Forbes gets a bum rap. Yes, it's true he has never worked for anyone but his father, the extravagant Malcolm Forbes, who was well known for his love of ballooning and collecting Fabergé eggs. But boy, was Malcolm lucky to have a son like Steve. Forbes magazine has prospered during his reign. In the 1996 and 2000 presidential races, the attempt to portray Steve Forbes as a loony supplysider who was touting a flat tax purely for his own benefit was ludicrous. Yet the impression persisted, even after he vowed to exempt himself from the benefits!

Whether you agree with his economic philosophy or not, you cannot come away from a discussion with Steve Forbes without realizing that he spends a great deal of time trying to figure out how to improve the economic and social benefits of our country.

FIND YOUR OWN ADVENTURE

My grandfather came to this country as an immigrant. He was one of ten children; he had a grade-school education and very little money. But he loved writing about how people shaped business and politics with their own style. He frequently wrote about the great shapers and entrepreneurs of his day. Eventually, he decided he wanted his own adventure and created his magazine.

My father and grandfather both, in a sense, showed me that, after you watch how things are done, you need to go out there and do them on your own. When I went to work at my father's magazine, he said to me, "Mine isn't the only way of doing things. Over time, develop your own way." He was hammering home the point that you shouldn't try to imitate others. And he was a trusted source on the topic, because he truly was one of a kind. He was a formidable figure and it would have been very easy to feel overshadowed by him. But my brothers and I learned from his example, even as we took care to develop our own styles. If you can do that, I realized, you'll have a chance at a good life. But if you let others try to shape your life, you're just going to be frustrated.

MAKE YOUR OWN MISTAKES

When we were growing up, my father was very strict. But as we became teenagers he knew how to let go. He knew how to give you enough room to make mistakes without destroying yourself. He did the same thing when I went to work at the magazine. For many years, I didn't work with him directly. He had worked for his father, so he knew the perils of that kind of relationship. So I worked for others, and from time to time I even took positions in direct opposition to his. That didn't bother him in the least. All he wanted to know was whether I had the ability to run a company.

What I learned from him was that the key to success is being passionate and interested in what you are doing. It isn't about following someone else's lead, it's about figuring out what you want and going for it.

PURSUE YOUR OWN VISION

I took over the company after my father died in 1990. There was considerable skepticism about my ability to take his place. I was not a balloonist. I was not a motorcyclist. Even today, I feel I'm too young for motorcycles. But I had a vision of where I wanted the company to go, and I decided that should I follow my father's advice and set my own precedents. If you have your own vision, pursue that vision. People will always come around.

QUIT COMPLAINING AND DO SOMETHING

I think that advice helped again when I made the plunge into politics during the 1996 presidential race. In 1995, when Jack Kemp decided not to run for president, I saw no other progrowth candidate out there. I thought, "Well, instead of just writing about it and complaining about it, go out there, get in the ring, and do something about it."

You've got to set the pace and the agenda. Have the vision and pursue it. I didn't win, of course, but I feel confident that the issues I brought to the table continue to be important. Even today, I hear John McCain talking about the issues I started discussing ten years ago. At the time they seemed very radical, outside the mainstream, but today they're front and center of the national debate. How to reform Social Security? How to change and simplify the tax code? How can you create health savings accounts and a differently structured health care? These are all questions I raised because I knew they were important. Now these issues are at the forefront of the national debate, and I think my campaign helped move them forward. Sure, it took longer for people to come around than I may have wanted, but hey—that's the way democracy works.

HAROLD FORD JR.

UNITED STATES CONGRESSMAN

★ ★ ★

Many say that Representative Harold Ford Jr. is the person who can fill the generation gap that exists within Democratic Party. His rise to power has been rapid: After earning his B.A., he became a special assistant to the United States Department of Commerce. After earning his J.D., in 1996 he won his retiring father's U.S. congressional seat at the age of twenty-six. More important, he won reelection with 84 percent of the vote. He was suggested as a vice presidential candidate in the 2004 election, but was ineligible because he was not old enough!

Harold Ford Jr. is a Democrat who began in Washington with a perfect 100 in an annual index of congressional liberalism. But many in both parties say that he has evolved from a tow-the-line-with-blinders-on partisan to a true leader willing to part with his party when he feels it is out of sync with the people he represents. His family name may have helped him make the first step in politics, but at this point he has certainly proven himself on his own merits. He ran against Representative Nancy Pelosi for House minority leader. While many urged him to bow out, he stayed in, arguing that centrist Democrats are the party's future. Representative Pelosi won, as everyone expected, but Representative Ford may have the bigger payday in the long run.

RUN HARD WHEN NO ONE IS WATCHING

The greatest advice in my life came from my father, Representative Harold Ford Sr., and my track coach from St. Albans, Skip Grant. St. Albans is a school with a lot of wealthy kids, and I wasn't a wealthy kid. For a long time, my track coach was the only black person on the school faculty, besides the folks who worked on the janitorial staff. But he was, safe to say, the most respected person on staff. He taught a class on character and coached the cross-country, track, and swim teams. He built us into young men.

One day, when I was in ninth grade, I was running the jogging loop around the school premises. When I came to the final part of the two-and-a-half-mile loop, where the coach was standing, I started running as fast as I could. Coach Grant jumped all over me. "You shouldn't just run fast when you're in front of me. It's when you're back there, where no one can see you, that you need to run fast. When you get in front of people you feel good, and of course you'll do well. Run hard, even if you're in last place at the finish. Run hard when people aren't looking." I knew he was right. Before that, I'd only run hard when I was trying to impress him. After that day, I tried to apply that lesson to everything I do in life. I try to always behave as I would if people were watching.

FAITH WILL HELP YOU THROUGH

A life in politics isn't easy. I learned this at an early age, when my father was wrongly accused of influence-peddling. He had to go to court, and it was incredibly scary to wait for twelve people to come back and say, "You know, you're right, he didn't do it." That was one of the single biggest moments of maturation in my life as we stood there and waited for the verdict to come back. I remember my father's courage and strength. I don't know how he kept his cool, but he did. I believe that his unshakable faith helped him through these trying times.

BUILD RELATIONSHIPS

When I ran for Congress the first time it was tough going, though I won in the end. I know that I benefited enormously from my dad's political reputation. But I also know that many local politicians did not support me. Rather, they tried to beat me. While my opponents were busy talking to the press, I was working behind the scenes. I met with every pastor in my district. I went to every school in my district and met with every principal, and I met with all the neighborhood and community organization leaders. I met with people the newspapers always forget to mention. I didn't spend my time wooing the richest people or the biggest donors in town. In fact, if you polled a hun-

dred of the most influential people in my city, I probably wouldn't have gotten more than three votes—if you presume my dad and two uncles voted for
me! While the rich people weren't looking, though, I was building important
relationships. And in the end it was these people I met with who actually
turned out to vote.

I campaigned when no one was looking, and that made all the difference.

GEORGE FOREMAN

TWO-TIME HEAVYWEIGHT CHAMPION OF THE WORLD

★ ★ ★

I wasn't sure what to expect when I first met George Foreman. His boxing come-back gives hope to anyone who wonders if they've passed their prime. I'd seen him on television selling his Lean Mean Grilling Machine; I figured he was just a guy who'd discovered an easy way to make a buck by lending his name to a product. Was I surprised! George walked into the green room with a huge smile on his face. I've since learned it's almost always there! He is so gregarious, you can't help but like him within minutes. But what really astounded me was when I started asking him about his grill. He went into depth about how terrific it was and how it would change my cooking style. He extolled its health benefits. And before long I realized that he was selling something he really believed in.

George gives new meaning to the term "hard worker." He's an ordained minister; you can often find him preaching at the Church of Lord Jesus Christ in Houston, Texas. He built the George Foreman Youth and Community Center. He is a family man . . . and I mean BIG family: He has five boys (all named George) and five girls (who escaped that tradition)! He is a businessman and author. Along with his grill line, he's also been responsible for a series of exercise tapes, cleaning products, a clothing line, and even inspirational CDs sung by George! For relaxation he escapes to his wild game ranch in the piney woods of Texas.

AGE DOESN'T MATTER

As a boy growing up in Marshall, Texas, I got into boxing in an odd way. My life wasn't going anywhere. I got in a lot of fights, at home and in street brawls. But then I saw a TV commercial saying, "If you dropped out of college and want a second chance, the Job Corps is for you." I joined, and a counselor there told me I should be a boxer. Soon I was skipping rope, running track, going for hikes. My whole life was rebuilt around boxing.

By 1968, I'd won the heavyweight gold medal at the Olympic Games held in Mexico City. The next year, as a pro, I had thirteen fights and won eleven by knockouts. By the end of 1971, I had a 32–0 record and was ranked as the number one challenger by the WBA and WBC. In 1973, I became the world champion with a second-round knockout of Joe Frazier. I left boxing in '77, but when I was forty-five I reclaimed the heavyweight title for a second time. I loved saying I was the oldest boxer ever to win the title. It proved my age didn't matter. At least that's what I thought.

NO ONE CAN EAT EXCUSES

I retired again, but later on I started thinking about making another comeback. I wrote to a boxing promoter, Henry C. Winston, to complain about what the newspapers and prospective promoters were saying about my age. He said, "George, no one can eat excuses." I asked him what he meant. In the old days down South, he explained, a farmer with a family to feed would go out squirrel hunting if he couldn't afford any other meat. His family would be ready and waiting, and if that farmer came back home he couldn't bring excuses—he had to bring home food.

That advice changed me in a lot of ways. When people said no, I learned, I had to find a way to make them buy what I was selling. I couldn't go home and tell my family, "I could have brought you some money back, but they said no," or "I could have paid for your college, but they didn't like me," or "They said I was old," or "I just couldn't get it done." One way or another, I was coming home with the food. I knew there were lots of promoters who were going to tell me no, and I had to sell them on the prospect that I was going to give them the best heavyweight fight ever, no matter what my age was. I learned to sit there and sell myself. If it took me three days or three weeks, I was going to come back with the bacon, so to speak. That advice served me well throughout my career. No one can tell me, "You're not a writer, George. You're not a television star, George. You're not a salesperson, George." I can achieve whatever I want—no excuses.

SELL YOURSELF

The only excuse for not selling is an excuse. Why shouldn't people buy a grill from George Foreman? It's not as if every salesman in America actually makes the product he sells; I haven't yet met a salesman who does. If a good salesman has a good product, he can sell it. To sell a product, though, you have to sell people on yourself first. I knew that if I made people love me, the first product they would buy is me. But if people detect insincerity, they'll stop and move on to someone else. You've got to make them love you.

SMILE

When I went into sales, I decided I was going to be selling twenty-four hours a day. If you commit to that, you can't miss. If you're a salesman for only eight hours a day, you're not going to get the prize. I've been on an airplane asleep in first class and people will walk through the airplane and shake me to wake me up. They'll say, "George Foreman, I have your grill. Will you sign this for me?" I wake up smiling and say, "Thank you so much," and tell them to keep grilling. Word of mouth travels better than any advertisement you can buy.

I don't sell half the day; I sell twenty-four hours a day. When I go through an airport, I'm tired. When I get off a bus, I'm tired. When I stop in at a gas station, I'm tired. But you must be a salesman to get the job done. If you can sell, you'll never starve. I constantly tell my kids, "Learn to sell, and you'll always have something to eat."

Senator William Frist and his father, Dr. Thomas Frist

WILLIAM FRIST

SENATE MAJORITY LEADER

In 2000, Senator Bill Frist was elected to his second term by the largest vote total ever received in a statewide election in Tennessee. Clearly, he's impressed the people of his state. But what impresses me so much about Bill Frist is that he is a doctor first and a politician second. Senator Frist released his book When Every Moment Counts *soon after the tragedy of September 11, as Americans were scrambling to comprehend how to safeguard themselves against the possibility of a bioterrorism attack. I read the book then, and have reread it several times since. I think everyone in America should have a copy. Instead of overwhelming you with too much information, Dr. Frist clearly and methodically answers the most common questions in a user-friendly way. You close the book having gained both knowledge and a greater peace of mind. It's comforting to know that someone in a high place in our government fully understands the threat we all face.*

HEALING IS A CURRENCY FOR PEACE

I get up every morning and look in the mirror and see a physician. But I am now also a citizen legislator. Spending time with people in Iraq, Afghanistan, India, Pakistan, and Sri Lanka has highlighted for me the link between my two careers, as a doctor and as a senator.

My dad was the man who gave me the philosophy that healing could be used as a currency for peace. He was a family physician and a humble man who practiced medicine for sixty years. He was originally from Mississippi but moved to Nashville, Tennessee, to practice. He felt there was no nobler calling than medicine; he felt it was the definitive public service.

FAITH AND CHARACTER

I'm the youngest of his five children. Not long ago, in a straightforward letter to his great-grandchildren, he spelled out the philosophy by which he lived. The specific advice is expressed through simple principles that he lived by. The letter opens with his talking about religion and faith, not in an excessively evangelical way, but in a way that shows the centrality of faith and spirituality, which provides guidance for everything else that you do. His second focus is on character and integrity throughout life.

I believe that a greater emphasis on principles like those would elevate the field of politics—which is important because the public, in some ways rightfully, thinks politics tends to bring out some of the very worst in people's characters.

THE CURVE IS ALWAYS GOING UP

There was an optimism that my father passed on to me. "Life is made up of peaks and valleys," he told me, "but the thing to remember is that the curve is always going up. The next peak is a little higher than the previous peak; the next valley isn't quite so low." This hopeful vision of life helps me whether I'm interacting with patients in a hospital in Afghanistan or talking to soldiers who are training Iraqis. It also affects my belief in democracy and peaceful transitions of government—the power of the individual vote. As my father wrote, "Think about politics—we'll get a bad president, and then a great president who corrects the things the other one did. That's a great thing about the party system." Look how they're coming out of the valley in Afghanistan and Iraq, where there is a very successful move toward democracy.

Lastly, my father stressed the importance of humility. It is reflected in the life of a physician, where you learn to put others first. Your doctor–patient relationship is built on a real trust and a focus on other people. By listening to other people, giving them a chance to talk, you can often arrive at a diagnosis pretty quickly, without a lot of testing or technology.

DON'T THINK ABOUT THE REWARD

What I learned from my father relates directly to my job as majority leader of the Senate. In this room, I focus on interpersonal relationships between a hundred United States senators. My goal is to capture the strength of each of those senators, minimize their weaknesses, and establish a common good, recognizing that every one of them brings a slightly different political bent to the conversation. My father told me, "Don't think about the reward; that will probably come along if you don't go looking for it." As a child, I was never the very best in my class at any one thing, so I never became arrogant or overconfident. I had to work hard, even if a reward wasn't anywhere in sight. To this day, I know it takes hard work, early mornings and late nights, to accomplish good things for other people.

WORK TO ELEVATE OTHERS BEYOND WHERE THEY ARE TODAY

My dad died a few years ago. Even though he tolerated my going into politics, he thought it was crazy. He said, "There is no greater profession than medicine—the healing art of a personal relationship with another that helps their lives to be preserved and fulfilled." Therefore, he was puzzled by the fact that I would want to spend my time in another form of public service. There were really only two times he was ever baffled with me. He wasn't really disappointed but he scratched his head. One is when I left the South to go to college in the Northeast. He felt there was no reason to leave the great state of Tennessee. The second was when I told him I was going to serve in the United States Senate. He asked, "Why in the world would you go into politics?" I was never sure he understood that my commitment to the Senate and my constituents comes from the exact same motivation that drives me to be a physician. They are both healing jobs. When I do a heart transplant or transplant someone's lungs, it doesn't just need to go well technically. My patients need to go on to live lives that are fulfilling, to be with their families, to have children, to go back to work, to have what they want.

That same healing process occurs for me here in the Senate. Every inter-action, or piece of legislation or bill, must help the world to get better, to be more fulfilling, and to elevate others beyond where they are today.

IT'S SATISFYING TO CHANGE THE COURSE OF HISTORY

One of the more common questions I get is, "As a surgeon, where your job is to cut out what's bad and put in what's good, how can you tolerate being in politics, where legislation is made like sausage and never comes out the way one intended?" I simply point to what I regard to be the single most im-portant moral public and humanitarian challenge of the last fifty years: the global HIV/AIDS crisis. It has killed 23 million people, 40 million people are infected, and another 60 million people are going to die unless we act. But through leadership and the legislative process, we have the opportunity to reverse that moral and humanitarian challenge, and we are doing so. The Senate has passed legislation to authorize $15 billion to help fund HIV/AIDS research and relief, and that money will help change the course of his-tory. That's pretty satisfying.

As hard as I work, I can only perform a certain number of surgeries a year. But imagine how many people I can help with one piece of good legis-lation. We have other huge challenges, both natural catastrophes and politi-cal crises. We can have the same impact if we go back to those basic principles, and—with humility and character—pull the very best out of people.

GO DO SOMETHING ELSE—THEN BRING YOUR EXPERIENCE WITH YOU

Another specific piece of advice I received came from Congressman Joe Evans of Tennessee. I was an intern here in 1972, and I saw the power of public policy to help people. At that time, I knew I was going to medical school. Both my brothers were doctors. My dad was a doctor. I was the last of five children signed on to be a doctor. Then, in college, I realized that it might possible to be both a doctor and a politician. I sat down and discussed it with Congressman Evans. He told me, "If I were you, I'd go do something else for twenty years—not in Washington, D.C., not in politics, and not in policy. Then bring that experience back to Washington." He said it doesn't matter specifically what it is you do, but that Congress is strengthened if people come from a variety of backgrounds and experiences.

In 1994, twenty years later, I won a seat in the Senate. Congressman Evans was right. My background gave me the insight to use medicine as a currency of peace. I am better able to address things like health care, which is the largest part of our economy and today affects every individual, and in-surance premiums, which are skyrocketing and making us less competitive globally. If I hadn't spent that twenty years taking care of patients and serv-ing others in the health care field, I wouldn't be able to be the voice that I am.

Kathie Lee Gifford and her parents

KATHIE LEE GIFFORD

TELEVISION PERSONALITY

★ ★ ★

You've seen Kathie Lee Gifford on all the big talk shows. Her CDs are bestsellers. She has her own clothing line. And she's a successful off-Broadway producer. But Kathie Lee is much more than her work.

In the 1990s, I was working at WABC-TV in New York City, anchoring the morning and noon news. The wildly popular show Live with Regis and Kathie Lee *shared the same studio, taping between my two shows, and for several years I would see Kathie Lee every day in the dressing and makeup rooms. I had the opportunity to see her interact with her staff, her assistant, and her fans. She was incredibly and genuinely friendly to the people who often mobbed her with photograph requests. At the end of each season, she would sell off her wardrobe to staff members and give the money to charity. I witnessed Kathie Lee's graciousness, generosity, and unconditional love for her children and husband. I hold her in very high regard.*

MAKE YOUR OWN MUSIC

My dad was the kind of parent who was constantly filming my brother, my sister, and me. He's got tape all of our little shows and recitals on those old-fashioned reel tapes. When I was five years old, I was singing "Mary Had a Little Lamb," and I stopped in the middle of singing and said, "Where's the music, Daddy?" On the tape you can hear my father say, "Oh, sweetheart, you have to learn to make your own music." That moment has touched me as deeply as anything in my life. I thought I knew what he meant, but I've been surprised at all the times those words have come back and taken on new relevance in my life. Decades later, when I started writing my own songs, writing the lyrics and bringing the melodies to life, those words of my father's were still an eye-opener.

Growing up, I was interested in French and in the theater. I also loved flowers, and for a while thought I would be a florist. I was talking to my dad about it one day, and he said, "Honey, find something you love to do, and then figure out a way to get paid for it. Where your passion lies is where your joy will be, and when your joy is combined with your passion you'll find the ultimate success."

BE A STUDENT THROUGHOUT YOUR LIFE

I truly enjoyed hosting *Live with Regis and Kathie Lee*. It was lucrative, and very few people would be tempted to walk away from that success. But I was in a wonderful velvet rut for fifteen years. When I finally had the strength to leave, I remembered something else my dad had told me: "Honey, if you can do something with your eyes closed, it's time to find something new." Right before I left the show, I realized that I wasn't being creatively challenged; I wasn't making my own music. I was making a fortune, but I wasn't doing something I enjoyed.

When I left the show, my father was dying and we didn't know how much time he had left. Everything came together at once. The thought of losing my father, who had always been an oak tree of a man, was difficult to bear. The song in the second act of my new play, *Under the Bridge*, was written on the day I flew to Delaware to bring my father home from the hospital to die. The lyric says, "Old Mother Nature is dressing in her cloak as the last leaf dances on the branches of the oak." As I was writing it, I happened to look out on my backyard. There was this huge oak tree with one leaf still dangling on the branch, just like my father. I just prayed that God would give me comfort—that I would never lose my daddy and he would always be with me, even though he was leaving me physically and I would never be able to hold him and hug him anymore. I can't describe what it has been like to see people moved by that song eight shows a week, and to think that even in death my daddy still has a tremendous influence in my life.

LIVE A GODLY LIFE

Fortunately, my daddy knew how inspirational he was in my life. My mom and I have become even closer since he passed away. What we both had in common is that we both loved the same man in different ways. He was just the most decent, Godly man. He didn't just teach me about a Godly life, he lived it. I look at how my life is full of joy and new challenges, and I know it's because of his advice.

ALBERTO GONZALES

UNITED STATES ATTORNEY GENERAL

★ ★ ★

I was standing in a slow-moving line in Washington, D.C., one evening when a friendly woman just ahead of me struck up a conversation. When I realized that Becky and I were both Texans, it became a very informal chat. I was just thinking about how much I missed women like her on the East Coast when our husbands walked up. I introduced Mr. Hill, and Becky said, "This is my husband, Al." When I took a good look at him, I realized why he looked so familiar: the big news story of the week was his recent nomination to replace John Ashcroft as U.S. attorney general.

If you didn't know he was a high-profile lawyer, you'd never have guessed it from his manner. Alberto Gonzales is warm, self-deprecating, and down to earth. Rather than talk about politics, Becky and Al will chat forever about their kids. In a town that can be crazy, they're a really normal couple.

Alberto Gonzales was working as a lawyer for the Houston firm Vinson and Elkins when he was named general counsel to then-Texas governor George W. Bush in 1994. He became the Texas secretary of state three years later, and was named to the Texas Supreme Court in 1999 (he won reelection a year later with 81 percent of the popular vote).

Gonzales is special because he's involved in more than just his career. He is also incredibly dedicated to his community: He has worked on local boards for the United Way, Leadership Houston, the Houston public schools, and the admissions committee for Rice University. He received the Presidential Citation from the State Bar of Texas for his dedication to addressing basic legal needs of the indigent. He is also the highest-ranked Hispanic American ever to serve in the U.S. government.

TO SUCCEED, YOU NEED AN EDUCATION

The people who gave me the advice that made the greatest impact on my life were two men stationed in Alaska with me.

I came from a pretty poor family. My parents weren't educated, so they were happy just to get me through high school and even happier when I graduated with honors from MacArthur High School in Houston. I enlisted in the service right away, without even considering going to college. I was sent to Fort Yukon, Alaska, and there I soon met these two Air Force Academy graduates. They told me about their experience at the Academy. "To succeed you need an education," they told me, "and there is no finer place to get that than at the Air Force Academy." Based on that, I was motivated to try.

One of the reasons I wanted to go to the academy was that I wanted a higher education. But I also had a dream of becoming a fighter pilot. With their help, and the help of others, I got the appointment. From there I transferred to Rice University, and then went on to Harvard Law School. It all started with those conversations in Alaska.

REALIZE YOUR DREAMS

I truly appreciate the time I spent at the Academy. It was a tough two years, but it was worth it. Not only are you getting a wonderful education, but you're guaranteed a job when you get out. Along the way, you learn about discipline and taking care of yourself.

It was only because of a dream I had that I ever considered leaving the Academy. When I was a boy, about the age of twelve or thirteen, I got a job selling soft drinks at Rice University football games. Normally, in the third or fourth quarter, you stopped selling drinks; by then people had quit buying, and by then Rice, being the team it was, was usually out of the game. Folks would lose interest and start going home. I'd watch the end of the football game, and then I'd climb to the top of the stadium and watch the students stroll back to their college dorms. As I watched them, I'd think about what it would be like to go to school there. From that moment on, I had the dream of being one of those students.

In my childhood, this was just a dream. But after I got to the Academy and started thinking about a transfer, I applied to only one school: Rice. I made the transfer and that's where I got my undergraduate degree.

VALUE HARD WORK

This is a generalization, but at a service academy I think you develop greater maturity, a sense of duty and unity, because you know you may be called upon to fight and defend your country, perhaps to give your own life for your country. That's a pretty sobering experience. I think you learn discipline, to take orders, to take care of yourself, Your life at a service academy is divided into three categories: academics, athletics, and military regimen, in which you learn military history, the military code, and obligations under the laws of war. That kind of life of service had an appeal for me.

My parents instilled in me the value of hard work. My dad probably worked harder than any person I ever knew. He went to work every day to provide for our family. He was a construction worker when I was younger, and later got a job on the maintenance crew at a rice mill. He was extremely responsible, because he felt that his number one job was to provide for his family in what he felt was a proper manner. For my parents, success wasn't a matter of the children going to college, because my mother had a sixth-grade education and my father a second-grade education. For them, a success was getting us through high school.

ROSEY GRIER

**FORMER NFL FOOTBALL PLAYER AND COFOUNDER
OF IMPACT URBAN AMERICA**

★ ★ ★

Anyone who ever watched a Los Angeles Rams football game in the early 1960s will remember the "Fearsome Foursome," which is often considered the best defensive line in the history of football. But who would have thought that Rosey Grier, the All-Pro defensive tackle, would one day be known for his expertise in macramé and needlepoint?!

He never was your typical football player. Rosey was a close friend to fellow idealist Robert F. Kennedy. In fact, in 1968 Rosey was at L.A.'s Ambassador Hotel with Bobby and Ethel, who was then pregnant with their eleventh child, when Bobby was killed just days before the Chicago Democratic National Convention. During the chaos after the shots rang out, Rosey managed to grab the killer's hand and pin him down.

Now an ordained minister and founder of a nonprofit resource center developing educational programs for disadvantaged teens, Rosey Grier is a man of intellect and honor.

TROUBLE IS EASY TO GET INTO AND TOUGH TO GET OUT OF

My dad once told me, "Trouble is easy to get into and hard to get out of." That advice became the foundation for the way I wanted to live my life. I wanted to stay out of trouble, because I knew it would hunt me and dog me and stay with me forever.

I remember one night when I was with some young men from my community. I said, "I'm not going, because I know you're looking for trouble." They didn't give me too much trouble, though. The worst they ever did was calling me "Goodie Two Shoes." Names didn't bother me—you know the old rhyme about sticks and stones. I was usually able to live by what I knew was right. Staying out of trouble was a code I lived by.

WHEN YOU MESS UP, CLEAN UP

My dad made it very clear what he expected from me. I was to be home from school by a certain time in order to help with work around the house. (Keep in mind that I had to beg to go to school in the first place.) Well, one day I got into a marble-shooting contest on the way back from school, and I got home late. My dad whipped me. Sometimes, if I got back late, he'd just say, "I owe you one." Inevitably, I would do something where I'd end up getting two whippings. One would be for the thing I had just done wrong. Then he'd say, "Remember I said I owed you one?" And I'd get both. That was a great deterrent to stay away from trouble.

Of course, every kid messes up sometime; so do adults. But I learned that when I did mess up, I should immediately try to clean it up so I wouldn't have to deal with it later. I don't want to walk around with a problem hanging over me. So if something comes up I've learned to face the problem right away, so I don't have to deal with it later. Get your problems taken care of right off the bat, as opposed to hiding from them. They'll always find you.

FIND WHAT IS GOOD FOR ALL

If you have a mission and you let distractions get in the way, you will not fulfill your mission. Foolishness will throw you off. Selfishness, and seeking what's easy for you instead of what's good for all, will throw you off. In sports, you learn how to work in a team. Each person on the team has a part to play, and if you don't play your part, the team is not going to win. If you do your part and encourage others to do theirs, it all gets done. No one is better than anyone else. It doesn't matter if you play quarterback or you're the mayor or you're the president, because everyone on the team is of the same importance.

When I look at the president, I look at him as our representative. But I'm also as responsible as he is for playing a part to make sure that things are accomplished for our country. He has opportunities to speak to more people, but I have more influence with the people I have occasion to see. I learned this through my association with Senator Robert Kennedy. We used to talk about how to make people in the nation think more highly of one another. When I wondered what a black ballplayer could say to make people respect each other, he helped me see that I could make just as much of an impact as anyone else.

It is with passion that I believe in this country, and in the rights of others. It is with passion I believe that no one is better than anyone else. The greatest athlete you've ever known is great for only a little while. The greatest leader of the world, for that matter, lasts only a little while. The president is only running the office the people chose him to run. That doesn't make him better than anyone else. It makes him a man we trust to lead us to a better place.

SPEAK OUT AGAINST EVIL

Another way people get themselves or others in trouble is by talking negatively. If people do that in front of me, I tell them I don't like it. I know that if I allow people to say negative things around me, they may conclude that I'm tacitly in agreement with them. Think about Sirhan Sirhan. What if there were people who knew that he'd started thinking about killing someone?

You need to speak out against evil. Suppose someone had told Sirhan Sirhan that killing is wrong, that in a democracy we don't solve things that way. Be an outspoken voice against negative or cruel or immoral people, and support those who represent more of what you want for society. Violence isn't the solution. People also talk negatively about others they don't even know. We shouldn't dislike people because they're black or white or brown or yellow. That's not the way you solve a problem. If you don't know somebody, get to know him and spend time with him rather than putting him down because he looks different or doesn't speak your language. Soon, you'll realize that we're all the same.

LIES KEEP CHANGING,
BUT THE TRUTH STAYS THE SAME

Remember the Bible story about Adam and Eve in the Garden of Eden? When they ate the apple from the tree of knowledge, they realized they were naked. When God asked why they were hiding, they replied, "Because we're naked." God asked Adam, "How do you know you're naked?" Well, immediately Adam started to blame Eve. It is man's tradition to try to pass the buck.

Recently, I was reading the story about the scribes and Pharisees coming to Jesus and asking why the disciples were breaking the rules of the Elders. Jesus asked them why they had those traditions, instead of following the traditions of God. Man always thinks that just because he does it, it must be right. But there's a right way and a wrong way to do things. If you do things the right way first, you won't have to deal with it later. You realize that the truth always stays the same, but lies are always changing. So you should tell the truth the first time; then you won't have to worry about anything. You'll keep telling the same story.

ALEXANDER HAIG

FORMER UNITED STATES SECRETARY OF STATE

★ ★ ★

Alexander Haig has spent his life trying to improve each situation he found him-self in. As a general during the Vietnam conflict, he commanded an infantry division. He returned stateside as a member of Dr. Henry Kissinger's National Security Council staff, and then was called on to help negotiate the final Vietnam ceasefire talks. President Richard Nixon appointed him chief of staff, and General Haig helped manage the crisis of Watergate. He continued in the position under President Gerald Ford. In 1974 he became the Supreme Allied Commander of NATO, and in 1981 he became secretary of state in President Ronald Reagan's cabinet. He has had a unique perch from which to observe history, and a challenging position from which to determine it.

DON'T MISTAKE HISTORIC CHANGE FOR CONTEMPORARY PROBLEMS

My life was changed by advice I received as a graduate student at Georgetown University, while seeking a master's degree in international relations. Professor James Atkinson warned me—and I've been guided by this warning ever since—"Don't mistake issues that are the product of historic change and ultimately become facts, for contemporary problems that require timely solutions."

For example, take the emergence of interdependence, or, in today's jargon, "globalism." This is a historic fact and not, as so many believe today, simply the product of conscious policy. Frequently, such facts do require adjustments to better preserve national interests, but they cannot be changed or reversed by simple policy shifts. Today, the emergence of globalism is a fact that must be dealt with as such. It cannot be modified by simple policy change.

It's not an easy concept for many people to grasp. In the 2004 presidential campaign, for example, the Democrats were constantly attacking the president for the flow of jobs outward. They complained that jobs were being exported in support of globalism. Well, that shows they don't understand that this is a historic fact. Globalism is not a policy. It is a fact with which we have to cope. You're just mistaken if you think you can change historic reality. You deal with it, but you can't change it. That's something we simply haven't learned here in America. That doesn't mean it doesn't require some shifts in policy to meet our national interests. But if people think this is a conscious policy by the Bush administration, and could be solved by a mere shift in policy rather than an historic reality, they are spinning their wheels.

COOPERATE, DESPITE THE RISKS

You cannot ignore globalism. The world is getting smaller; there's no way of stopping that. You can't be like the libertarians, like Pat Buchanan, who think that we have the luxury of cutting ourselves off from this reality. The world is more interdependent, and we have to participate in ways that are in our best interest. As the world becomes more global in character, and former geographic and boundary changes are less significant, we have to have some universal, or global, approaches to policy change, rather than try unilaterally to affect reality. It means more cooperation, despite the great risks that it brings.

DON'T TILT AT WINDMILLS

It was a professor who made me realize the importance of shifting the way people view the world so that they can more clearly approach national and international issues. This taught me to be very careful about differentiating between global facts, which you must factor into decision making, and global problems, which can be solved by adjusting policy. There are a number of contemporary problems, such as world hunger, that are a product of simple fact, rather than a product of wrong-headedness. Those that are a product of fact have to be dealt with one way, and those that are a product of improper policies have to be dealt with another way. If you don't discriminate between the two, you get yourself in very serious trouble. That's what Don Quixote tended to do—tilt at windmills.

Understanding this concept is the art of foreign affairs, which too few of the contemporary critics in our legislature, popular opinion, and media understand. They simply are not sorting out facts from problems. It deprives us of precision in the conduct of foreign affairs, which can lead to very serious misjudgments and disappointments. In other words, trying to change a fact is always going to fail, because the fact is a fact and can't be changed. It has to be dealt with, but it can't be reversed.

Rebecca Huffman and her father, Lee Agnew, 1946

REBECCA HUFFMAN

TEACHER

I hold no higher regard than for great teachers. They are rare. A great teacher is one who crosses the line from simply instructing on a subject, to breathing life into that subject—and, in the process, making the student alive. As you'll read here, Mrs. Huffman, my biology teacher at Dripping Springs High School, did that for me—and more. Through her inspiration, I developed a lifelong passion for marine biology. But she also became the one adult other than my parents whom I could turn to for advice, guidance, and a shoulder to cry on. (In high school, after all, a breakup with a boyfriend felt like the end of the world!) I spent hours and sometimes weekends with her, talking and laughing and learning about life. When I put on the ubiquitous fifteen pounds my freshman year of college, she was the only one to tell me to my face that I looked fat and to go on a diet. That takes a very strong friendship. Later, at the most sensitive times in my life, I often turned to her for help and advice. She was always there for me, and she had the same incredible relationship with a number of other students. She not only changed our lives—she made them more.

ALWAYS BE ABLE TO FORGIVE, AND NEVER HOLD A GRUDGE

Each experience in our life influences us in some way, whether positive or negative—every one of them. These stand out in my mind:

My mother gave me guidance throughout life, teaching me forgiveness and always to be nondiscriminatory. As a result, my life has been blessed by always being able to forgive, and never being inclined to hold resentments, grudges, or hatred.

My father had no sons, just me, his only daughter. He blessed me in many ways. He taught me how to fish, took me to many baseball games and movies, and, most of all, took me hiking in the mountains of West Virginia. He had very little education, yet he knew most of the trees and would point them out to me, telling me of their economic importance. In the winter, he and I would hike into the mountains, dig up native dogwood, redbud, and hemlock trees, and transplant them in our front yard. It was my dad who gave me the interest in the natural biological world that led to my lifelong career teaching the biological sciences for a happy and productive thirty-three years.

By studying my supervising teacher, Rebecca Cole, I learned to be a master teacher. She was inspirational and so gifted in both the biological sciences and the total educational process that she influenced my teaching style. Three years ago, another teacher and I went back to West Virginia to see her, now in her eighties. It was still a wonderful, fulfilling experience to be with her.

Students taught me how to retain my youth. They blessed me by making me laugh and showing their appreciation for the knowledge they mastered. Many have kept in contact with me all their lives. One of the most fulfilling experiences I've had lately was being invited, by a student of thirty-five years ago, to go on a daylong wildflower outing with his family. It was such an intrinsic reward: Seeing his teenage children identifying the wildflowers along the highway, I witnessed how the knowledge I had shared with him had been passed onto his children.

The influence of a couple of friends can't be understated—including some who are my seniors by twenty years or more. Watching them taught me that growing old didn't have to happen. I had watched my parents grow negative and sedentary as they grew older, and thought that was life's natural progress. These two friends, however, had a motor home and traveled all over the United States and Canada. They went bird-watching throughout the world, always laughing, remaining positive, and having fun. They are in their mid-eighties now—but to me they are not old, nor will they ever be.

FLY YOUR KITE

Although we naturally think of the humans who have changed our life, I also think of something of a nonliving nature. A kite . . . yes, a kite. When I was a very young child, my parents took me to Virginia to see some ex-neighbors. One of them, Joe, had made an enormous airplane-shaped kite, and we all walked it up a hill for its first flight. The kite soared so very high that it just appeared as a tiny dot in the sky. Joe indicated that he might not be able to get the kite back down, because of its high altitude. Then he looked at me, a six-year-old, and said that if I got the kite down he would give it to me. I got it. I held this kite in my hands in the back seat of our automobile for the many hours of our return trip. At home I kept it in my bedroom, never flying it again for fear that something might happen to it. Many years passed with my kite stored away up high for safety. One day something fell on the kite and it was ruined—totally destroyed. It taught me a lesson. You see, I never flew my kite—never got to see the soaring beauty of it or have fun with it . . . for fear of losing it. I lost it anyway. Many years later, I realized that much of my life had been spent living the very same way, and I had missed opportunities to enjoy life fully. Now, when I get the opportunity to try something new, I tell myself, "Go and fly your kite." And I've never missed another opportunity.

So I have been "flying my kite" more and more. I am turning sixty-five in a few months. This year I have been up in hot air balloon rides, I've flown on looping gliders, I've ridden out into the desert at dusk on a Harley Davidson motorcycle. I am living. Fully.

Kaye Bailey Hutchison and her mother

KAY BAILEY HUTCHISON

UNITED STATES SENATOR

★ ★ ★

Texas women are strong, independent, and reliable. Plus, in my eyes, they always have good hair days!

Senator Kay Bailey Hutchison fits that definition to a tee. As a girl growing up outside Austin, one of my favorite things to do on a date (no joke) was to stop by Whataburger, then drive to the capital building and walk around looking at the statues and paintings. My mother worked as a staffer for the legislature, and I could think of no life more exciting than that of a representative of the people. I loved politics so much that when most kids went off to sports summer camps, I was honored to represent my school at Girl's State (a camp that teaches young people about government) and ran for treasurer because the most powerful woman in Texas at that time was the state treasurer, Ann Richards.

Since then, I've met Senator Hutchison, the first woman to represent Texas in the U.S. Senate. You can't pigeonhole her. She's a no-nonsense former college cheerleader, a University of Texas law school graduate who became a television reporter, and a working mom who sponsored and passed legislation expanding retirement funds for stay-at-home spouses. She's sweet as the day is long, but tenacious when it comes to protecting rape victims' identities, or securing health care benefits for veterans. She's the kind of woman I hope my daughter will emulate as she grows up.

THINK DIFFERENTLY

I hit my first brick wall in life when I graduated from law school. I couldn't get a job. The top law firms in Houston and Dallas didn't hire women. For four months I went door-to-door trying to get someone to hire me. I was very disappointed and really down. I just thought, "My goodness, I've got my law degree that I worked so hard for, and I may not be able to get a job."

One of my friends said, "Have you ever thought about doing something that isn't law but maybe used your law knowledge in a different way?" That started me thinking.

Then, as I was driving home from yet another interview, I passed the television station in my neighborhood. I just drove right in, walked up to the secretary, and told her I'd like to talk to someone about a job. She asked, "What kind of job?" And I said, "News reporter." The news director came out and talked to me. "Well, we've never had a female reporter," he said, "and we've never had a reporter who's a lawyer. Maybe it's time." They didn't have a job opening, so they needed approval from the company owner. The station, as it happened, was owned and run by a woman—Oveta Culp Hobby. She said that KPRC-TV should be the first station in Houston with a female news reporter, and I was hired.

None of it would have happened if I hadn't received that pivotal advice from my friend to think differently. We all should have goals, but we also need the flexibility to say, "Okay, I didn't get what I want that way. So let's look for a different route."

NEVER GIVE UP

I've been knocked down a lot. When you're breaking barriers, you lose a lot. I've lost a lot of things I wanted in my life, including elections. My dad always said, "Never give up. If you persevere and work hard, you'll eventually be successful." He had been an insurance salesman early in his career, and he got used to getting turned down. But that never got him down, he said, because he knew that if he kept trying, he'd win the next contract.

LEARN HOW TO OVERCOME YOUR SETBACKS

I can't think of one successful person who hasn't faced setbacks. Often, the people who are successful early in life don't end up being the most successful people later on, because they didn't learn how to overcome setbacks. I actually read an article that said that the most successful people are the ones who face setbacks and prevail by relying on a great support network. For example, if a teenage girl faces rejection from a boy, she will feel devastated. But if her parents say something like: "You know, it's not the end of the world that one boy broke up with you. He wasn't right for you," she'll feel the encouragement and support, overcome her setback, and ultimately be a stronger person for it.

IT CAN'T BE ALL ABOUT YOU

Still, I don't think that girls are well prepared in our culture to handle losing. In politics, it's especially hard for women to learn that. Growing up, my friends and I all wanted to be popular and active in school. If you weren't elected class favorite, well, there was something wrong with you. Girls have to get over that, because in politics it can't be all about you. As a candidate, you have to run on issues, and you win or lose on those issues. I've lost elections, and I've had terrible things said about me. But I had wonderful parents, and they always supported me. Their support helped me realize that you can't give up.

RANDY JACKSON

AMERICAN IDOL JUDGE AND MUSIC PRODUCER

★ ★ ★

Some people are good enough to make it as musicians; others find their niche on the business side of the industry. Randy Jackson did it all. The best way to describe him is as a great guy with a big heart. On American Idol, *he's known for peppering his reactions with "Dawg," a word that reveals his Louisiana drawl. Working first, as a bass player for the rock band Journey, then later as a successful record company producer and executive with Columbia Records and MCA Records, Randy knows his stuff; on the show, contestants value his knowledgeable opinions—and his ability to know talent when he sees it.*

WHATEVER YOU DO, DO IT WITH CONVICTION

In college, an influential teacher said to me, "Whatever you do in life, whether you do it well or do it poorly, do it with conviction, so that people will see you're trying, and that your intentions are coming from your heart."

You know what that means: Even if you play an instrument really badly, play it loud and proud! That advice is so important, because it prepares you to attack life. It teaches you to go all out, instead of being timid. When I'm judging people on *American Idol,* I look for that conviction. I think you can really tell if people are giving it everything they've got, or if they're holding back their voice or their presentation because they're shy. You've always got to think, *This could be my one shot.* That's what my teacher was saying: that you have one chance to impress someone with what you can do. Are you going to go for it, or are you going to be hesitant? Do you want to be stuck later on wishing you'd said this or done that?

You may never get that shot again, so give it all you've got—every time.

ALPHONSO JACKSON

UNITED STATES SECRETARY OF THE DEPARTMENT
OF HOUSING AND URBAN DEVELOPMENT

★ ★ ★

In March 2004, the U.S. Senate unanimously confirmed Alphonso Jackson as the nation's thirteenth secretary of the Department of Housing and Urban Development. Among his previous jobs, he'd been the head of the Dallas Housing Authority, which consistently was ranked one of the best-managed big-city housing agencies in the country. Against all odds, Secretary Jackson has become one of the most influential people in the country. He holds himself to very high standards, and expects the same from everyone around him. He believes that when you expect more of people, you get more in return. Having marched with Dr. Martin Luther King Jr. to demand equality, today he stresses that with equal opportunity comes equal responsibility.

OUR ONLY LIMITATIONS ARE IN OUR MINDS

I was the last of twelve children. My father had a fifth-grade education, and my mother was a nurse midwife with an eleventh-grade education. My father always told me, "You can succeed, because the only limitation to your ability is in your mind."

But he also informed me that I would face racism in this country. "There are two ways in which you can view racism," he explained. "You can view it as a wall too high to get over, too deep to get under, or too wide to get around, and at that point you become a victim and you justify being in that position. Or you can view racism as a series of hurdles you have to jump, from birth until death." He said, "If you hit one of those hurdles, try to land on your back, because if you can look up, you can get up." I think that was the most important thing he and my mother taught me: that during life you're going to have setbacks, but never view a setback as something that stops you from progressing. "A setback is simply a setup for a comeback," they told me.

POOR IS A STATE OF MIND, NOT A CONDITION

When I was at Lincoln University in Pennsylvania, I called my mother one day after a sociology class and I asked her, "Why didn't you tell me we were poor?" She said, "You're not poor." I told her that the professor showed us a pyramid, and said that if you were down near the bottom and your father made less than this amount of money, you were poor. So she said, "Let me ask you some questions, son. Did you have a bike?" I said, "Yeah." She said, "Did you go to Catholic school?" I said, "Yeah." She said, "Did you ever miss a meal?" I said, "No." And she said, "Well, then you're not poor, and you go tell that professor he's wrong." She explained that poor is a state of mind, not a condition. The condition is poverty. There are plenty of wealthy people with a poor state of mind, so they're poor. They might not be poor economically, but they are poor.

EDUCATION, EDUCATION, EDUCATION

Just as my parents predicted, I did face a lot of racism. I grew up in Dallas at a time when the city still had colored and white water fountains. Blacks couldn't eat at Dallas lunch counters, and we went to segregated schools. I went to a black Catholic high school that was originally called St. Peter's Academy for the Colored back in the early thirties. Then it became St. Peter's Preparatory Academy. It was unusual in the sense that all the students were black, but all the teachers were white nuns and priests.

Even with the challenges of the era, my mother and father stressed that you have to believe in yourself and not become a victim. Despite his limited education, my father was very well read; he could quote you any passage from Shakespeare's writings. But the fact that he didn't have a formal education led him to be obsessed with the importance of securing an education for his kids.

In part, he was obsessed because he looked around and saw black people consistently talking about what they couldn't do. He said to me, "Yes, we *can* do it. Sure, people are going to stand in your way. You can either let them stand on your wings and hold you down, or you can carry them with you."

My mother and father did a phenomenal thing in educating all twelve of us. Think of it: a person in this country with a fifth-grade education facing racism and segregation, yet firmly believing that the most important thing for his children was education, education, education. As my father said, "Once you have it in your mind, you can't have it taken away from you."

GO TO SCHOOL TO LEARN

The only time I really questioned my father's beliefs was when I graduated from high school. I was All-American in track and my father refused to let me take a scholarship to Stanford or USC. "You're going to school to learn," he told me. "You can run track, but at no point will that be your primary purpose for being there." I ended up taking an academic scholarship to Lincoln College in Pennsylvania, but I still ran and became an All-American in college, too.

At seventeen, I will tell you that I thought my father was probably the meanest person I'd ever come in contact with because he wouldn't let me go to USC or Stanford. But today I realize he was brilliant. I'm convinced that if I'd gone out to California I probably wouldn't have graduated, because I would have been running after girls all the time. He knew that I wasn't mature enough to deal with that situation—and he was absolutely right.

TAKE RESPONSIBILITY

Unfortunately, it is uncommon to find black people who will stress the importance of education and taking responsibility. Bill Cosby has spoken out about taking responsibility, and he is absolutely correct. I had the chance to be with him this past summer and I think he was absolutely shell-shocked with the responses he got when he started telling black people they needed to take responsibility. The liberal community that Bill Cosby had always identified with turned on him immediately.

I said to him, "As a Republican who is black, welcome to the club. If you don't think monolithically like those so-called 'civil rights leaders,' then they think something must be wrong with you." Lately, some in the black community have stressed everything but education. As an example, look at athletics. Most people do not know that in our country, there are roughly four million grade school and high school athletes. When you get to college it's about three hundred thousand athletes. But we have fewer than eight thousand professional athletes. So the chance of a young black male becoming a professional athlete is very, very limited. You have a greater chance of becoming a doctor or lawyer if you study. We have not stressed that, especially with black males. I gave the commencement address at Hampton University before twelve hundred graduates. Nearly eight hundred of the graduates were black women. What has happened to the black male? We have not stressed how important it is to get an education. It's not enough just to talk about racism. Some of the problems, as Bill Cosby pointed out, have nothing to do with racism at all. They have to do with our not being prepared to face the greater world. If you're prepared, racism can be an impediment. But it cannot stop you from achieving. That's the way I see life.

WITH EVERY RIGHT, THERE IS A RESPONSIBILITY

Why aren't more people taking responsibility for what happens to their lives? Because they've bought into the theory of victimization. It has become politically correct to become a victim. That disturbs me tremendously.

When you think about the difficulties I faced growing up in Dallas—and yet I'm sitting here today as the secretary of the United States Department of Housing and Urban Development—it shows you how great this country can be if you prepare yourself. But many black people have bought into the victimization theory—more so than any group I've known. Many people have bought into the civil rights era philosophy that everything that occurs to us is because of the white man. Even if we decide to destroy each other, kill each other, not educate ourselves, it's not our fault. It's the white person's fault. That is absolute nonsense. Every person, black or white, must take responsibility for all of their acts.

As my father used to say, "With every right you have, there is a responsibility. If you don't want to take the responsibility, don't accept the right." I have run the public housing authority in Dallas, St. Louis, and Washington, D.C. I remember talking to a legal aid lawyer who told me that because I was a black, middle-class man he was shocked at my insistence on holding public housing residents responsible for their actions. I told him, "I believe that everyone, whether they are in public housing or other housing, is a human being with the same sense of worth I have. I expect each person to take care of his property." I wasn't willing to be paternalistic and patronizing just because they were low-income.

It was a very difficult position to take: liberals (both black and white) thought I was a right-wing nut, because I was saying that residents had to take care of their property or I was going to move them out. If I had treated the residents as victims, they would have acted as victims. Just look at public housing in a number of our cities: It has become a haven for people who prey upon others. That was something I was not going to have. If you demand responsibility from people, on the other hand, I believe that you will get it.

IT'S NOT IMPORTANT HOW LONG THE JOURNEY IS—FINISH IT

I have always believed in possibilities for every human being. When I was seventeen years old, I had a unique opportunity: I left college and went to Selma, Alabama, to work on voter registration at the request of Bernard Lee, one of the people closest to Dr. Martin Luther King Jr. We spent two months there, and I made both marches from Selma to Montgomery. The first attempted march, which was March 7, 1965, became known as "Bloody Sunday." We didn't make it. Troopers met us with nightsticks, tear gas, and dogs. I ended up being beaten alongside John Lewis and others. I still have the scars from the dog bite I got on my left leg. But we didn't give up and we marched again. At the state capital in Montgomery, Dr. King made what I consider to be his most important speech. "It is not important how long the journey is," he said. "What is important is that we finish it. If you have the belief that you will finish it, that in itself makes the journey worthwhile." That's the way I feel. If you respect human beings, then you should try to encourage them. You shouldn't in any way denigrate them or be paternalistic and patronizing to them.

CONTINUE TO CHANGE FOR THE BETTER

If you want to know how great this country is, think about this: I was born in a segregated community and went to segregated schools. I've seen this country change tremendously within the short period of time that I've lived on this earth. Whatever problems this country has, Americans always try to rectify them. Are they all rectified? No, but we're still trying. The journey we've taken from slavery to Condoleezza Rice, Colin Powell, Rod Paige, and me serving as members of the president's cabinet speaks volumes. I've had a chance to live in Africa, China, India, and Brazil, and every time I land back on American soil, I simply say, "God bless America." We are the freest people of color on the face of the earth. To me, that says a lot about the vision of this country. Think how quickly we got from where we were as a society in 1865 to where we are today. That's a phenomenal testament to this country. Has it always been easy? No. The point is, we have changed—and will continue to change—for the better.

BOB JOHNSON

FOUNDER, BET (BLACK ENTERTAINMENT TELEVISION)

★ ★ ★

With a background in history and a master's degree in public administration from Princeton, Bob Johnson didn't plan on becoming a media mogul. He's the type of person who got where he is by making friends and taking calculated risks. He is the founder of BET—Black Entertainment Television—which at last count reaches more than 65 million homes in the U.S. It became the first black-controlled company to be listed on the New York Stock Exchange. By believing in his own ability and putting himself on the line, Bob Johnson became a billionaire—and a leader in the African American community.

MAKE YOUR FRIENDS BEFORE YOU NEED THEM

In my early twenties, I was working on Capitol Hill as a press secretary to Walter Fauntleroy, a congressional delegate from the District of Columbia. One evening, I was speaking to a woman at a party, and she told me, "You'd make a good lobbyist for the cable television industry." I told her I didn't know anything about cable television, and she said she hadn't either until she began working with it.

She introduced me to Robert Schmidt, who was the president of the National Cable Television Association, and he hired me to lobby for the deregulation of the cable industry. When I asked Bob how I should approach the job, he told me something that I'll never forget: "Bob, make your friends before you need them."

BE WILLING TO WORK FOR YOURSELF

It was an exciting time to be a staff lobbyist for cable TV; the industry was expanding rapidly, and I had a chance to meet all the guys who were pioneering cable television. One person I remember was John Malone. At that time he was the CEO of the third largest cable company, which was called TCI. John and I have completely different politics; John is to the right and I'm on the left. But we liked each other, and we started talking. Despite our political differences, we found that we shared the same core values. We believed in entrepreneurial spirit, hard work, and a willingness to be your own boss. He believed in people, and he supported the idea of an entrepreneurial individualist. As you might imagine, we had some interesting discussions. One day Bob said, "Look, if you ever get some ideas about a business, come see me." So I said, "Okay," and I filed it in the back of my mind.

GET REVENUES UP, KEEP COSTS DOWN

About two years later, around 1980, I got the idea to start Black Entertainment Television. I put together a little two-sheet proposal on the idea, and I flew out to Denver to talk with John Malone. "John, this is what I want to do: I want to start a cable programming channel that targets African Americans," I told him. "I think it'll work, because African Americans are heavy consumers of television." When I finished my sales pitch, John—being the kind of guy who believes in entrepreneurs—asked, "Bob, how much do you need to start this business?" I said, "John, I'll need five hundred thousand dollars." This took place in all of thirty-five or forty minutes. He replied, "I'll tell you what I'm going to do. I'm going to buy 20 percent of your company for $180,000, and I'll loan you $320,000. In this deal, you'll be 80 percent and I'll be 20 percent." John didn't know it, but if he had reversed the numbers and said he'd take eighty percent and give me twenty, I still would've said, "That's a deal."

So Malone called in his lawyer and wrote me out a check for half a million dollars. It was more money than I'd ever seen in my life. I grew up in a working-class family with ten siblings. A half-million dollars was all the money in the world. As I was getting ready to leave, I asked, "By the way John, I've never run a business before. What advice can you give me?" I already had the check in my hands, so I figured it couldn't hurt to ask. He responded, "Bob, it's simple. Get your revenues up and keep your costs down." That was it for me. That was my Harvard Business School lesson! Years later,

I asked John why he didn't change the numbers. "You put up all the money," I said. "Yes, it was my idea but it was your money." I was in my late twenties; he was taking a real risk. He said, "Bob, I always knew you would work harder for yourself than you would for me."

PEOPLE PREFER TO DO BUSINESS WITH PEOPLE THEY LIKE

One thing I've learned in business is that most people, if given a choice, would prefer to do business with people they like. They'll do a deal with the devil if they don't have a choice, but if they do, they'd rather do a deal with you. Everyone wants to make some money, but it's also important to have some fun. That's why the best deal is one that not only makes good business sense, but is also the foundation for a friendship. John Malone and I made several deals after BET. He was my partner when I built a cable franchise in Washington, D.C., and he was my partner when we bought a cable franchise in Denver, Colorado, where he lives. It's been a great relationship.

And, since John never sold a single share of stock, when I sold BET to Viacom a few years ago, his $180,000 investment netted him $850 million.

Jim Keyes and Uncle Lenny

JIM KEYES

PRESIDENT AND CEO, 7-ELEVEN

★ ★ ★

To understand Jim Keyes, consider what he said when he received the Horatio Alger Award, honoring people who have achieved success despite enormous adversities. "The American dream isn't about being the richest man alive," he said. "It's about sharing the richness life has to offer and being an inspiration to others."

I met Jim just after I graduated from college. He was a groomsman in my wedding. To say that Jim faced an uphill climb in life is more than an understatement. His childhood home in Massachusetts lacked heating and indoor plumbing. When he was five years old, his parents split up and he moved in with an older sister. He later moved back in with his father until the town condemned their house. After that, he moved into his mother's trailer home. Throughout high school and college he worked almost seventy hours a week at McDonald's.

Yet Jim says that the adversity he faced in his life was an advantage. His parents may have had no money, he says, but they understood the richness of life. In that sense and many more, Jim Keyes is a very rich man.

EDUCATION WILL LEAD TO A LIFE
NO ONE ELSE CAN GIVE YOU

I grew up in North Adams, Massachusetts, with three brothers, two sisters, and no money. My parents never graduated from high school, and neither did most of my siblings. At a very early age, I saw the limitations they faced because they weren't educated. My father said to me, "An education will lead to a life we could never give you."

The one person in my family who had gone to college was my Uncle Lenny, who had become a teacher in western Massachusetts. I remember visiting him as a young boy and being awed by his library. In my young mind, I associated his library with his having gone to college. Then, about eight years ago, my wife, Margo, and I visited my aunt and uncle at their home. When we drove up to Uncle Lenny's simple frame house, I was struck by how small it seemed. In your memory, everything seems so much bigger than it does in reality. When we walked into the house, I said, "Uncle Lenny, I'd like to show Margo your library." My aunt and uncle looked at each other with puzzlement and asked, "What library?" Then, after some thinking, Uncle Lenny brought me to the tiny utility room. There, above the washer and dryer, was one shelf with a handful of books on it. "You don't mean this?" he asked. I realized that that was the only library I'd known as a child. But its size didn't matter; that little collection was a big influence on my childhood.

WHERE YOU START DOESN'T LIMIT WHERE YOU CAN GO

As a child, I realized that people with educations were able to do more, and enjoy more freedom, in their lives. My mother and father were intelligent people, and probably could have done some great things if they'd gotten an education. I think they both wanted to see me able to enjoy more. Uncle Lenny gave me the confidence to realize that it was possible for someone with my background to go to college. After college, I went on to business school at Columbia University in New York City. When I first started at Columbia, I had no real role models within the business world. The only companies I knew were the factories where my mother and father worked. But I happened to attend Columbia with the son of Sandy Weill, who was running Shearson Loeb Rhoades at that time. I learned from Sandy that he too had started from very humble beginnings. He told me, "Where you start doesn't limit where you can go."

Sandy shared with me how he had gone from being a runner on Wall Street to running a major corporation. He was a living example of the American dream fulfilled. It was after talking with him that I began to see a future for myself in business. I don't think Sandy sees himself as a mentor to me, but he was. At our graduation, Sandy taught me another powerful lesson. My brother, who is a truck driver, came to the ceremony wearing his powder blue leisure suit and cowboy boots—he definitely looked out of his league. At one point, I looked up and my brother was deep in conversation with

Sandy. This fascinated me. Frankly, though, I wondered what the two of them had to talk about! When I asked my brother, he said, "The transportation industry." It was just another reminder that it can be an advantage to come from humble beginnings. Sandy was just as comfortable talking to my brother, the truck driver, as he would have been talking to an investment banker.

LEARN TO ADAPT, HAVE CONFIDENCE, AND KEEP IT SIMPLE

After working for years in marketing and business strategy, I was named CEO of 7-Eleven in my early forties. Although I probably shouldn't say it, my reaction after the first six months was, "Now what do I do? Just grow shareholder value? Is that what it is all about—just making money?"

Soon after, I had a powerful dream. In the dream, I was shown that I had three gifts. First, I was able to adapt to change. Second, I had confidence that I could succeed. And third, I had the gift of simplicity. I don't see myself as extremely bright, but I can take very complex things and break them down into simple terms—perhaps just so that I can understand them! When I woke up, I thought about my role as CEO of 7-Eleven, and I realized that it gave me a wonderful platform from which to use my gifts to help others succeed. So I decided that I would help coach and inspire others within my company to achieve their own success. It also inspired me to create a foundation, called Education is Freedom, that helps people with challenged backgrounds and shows them that they can control their own destinies by getting an education.

DR. HENRY KISSINGER

FORMER UNITED STATES SECRETARY OF STATE

★ ★ ★

I have the wonderful opportunity to go to work each day and meet the most fascinating and influential people in the world; even better, I can satisfy my curiosity by asking them about whatever piques my interest.

In this light, Dr. Henry Kissinger presents a problem for me. I'd really like to have him on the show every day, because I'd never run out of things to ask him about. He's held so many varied positions, experienced so much, and has frequently been at the center of the most sensitive international negotiations. I'm always worried he'll get tired of being peppered with questions about the Mideast, Watergate, intelligence, various political leaders, and closed-door diplomacy and tell me to quit bothering him! Fortunately, he hasn't done that yet.

WHEN SOMEONE LOSES FAITH, THEY ARE READY TO BELIEVE ANYTHING

In 1944, when I was a private in the army, I was sent to Camp Claiborne in Louisiana for infantry training. There I met another private who, like me, was a refugee from Germany—though this private had left by choice, and I, being Jewish, had left out of necessity. He was thirty-eight and had two Ph.D. degrees. I was nineteen and had two years of night college. His name was Fritz Kraemer, and he was the greatest influence of my formative years.

One day, the general in charge of our 84th Infantry Division had Kraemer dress up in a German uniform, complete with monocle and riding crop, and give a speech to the rest of us about the moral and political stakes of war. Afterward, I did something I had never done before: I wrote him a letter and told him how impressed I was by his talk. A few days later—now dressed in his American uniform, but still carrying the riding crop and wearing the monocle—Fritz found me during training and invited me to have dinner with him.

When he asked me what I was studying, I told him that I was studying accounting at City College in New York. We spoke about my views and his values, and he told me, "You have one of the best political minds I've ever encountered, and you ought to work in political science." He continued, "If you go and complete your training with a good attitude, I will find you."

A month after my division reached the front line, Fritz pulled me back to the G-2 intelligence section. We worked together, and over the next decade he shaped my mind in manifold ways. He influenced my reading choices, my thinking, and my choice of college. He even inspired my graduate theses. He once said, "Intellectuals have always preached that everything is relative and that there are no absolute values. . . . The result is spiritual emptiness. Everything is possible, and therefore nothing is. The worst thing about a loss of faith is not the fact that someone has stopped believing, but that they are ready to believe anything." He was a devout conservative, and I agreed with him that we had to fight communism. But I could not follow the absolutist strategy that he insisted on. Later on, I would be attacked by the liberals for fighting communism too much, and by conservatives for being too flexible. Fritz Kraemer didn't speak to me for the last thirty years of his life, because he thought I was insisting on negotiation, while he preferred confrontation. There was no hostility between us. I had a job to do, which was to help steer America through cataclysms while preserving an option for peace. At the same time, he had absolute values to keep. Despite our differences, I spoke affectionately at his funeral.

THINK

At the height of the Cold War in 1953, I was at Harvard as a graduate student. At that time I was working on early nineteenth-century European history, and I was going to write a book on the making of peace after the Napoleonic wars until the outbreak of World War I. I'd also spoken on campus a bit about foreign policy. One day, I was walking across Harvard Yard and ran into Arthur Schlesinger Jr. He gave me a letter that he had received from the secretary of the Air Force, Thomas Finletter, regarding nuclear weapons and the then-dominant strategy of massive retaliation. He asked me, "What do you think?" In response, I wrote Arthur a memorandum on the problems of massive retaliation.

Unbeknownst to me, he sent my memo to the editor of *Foreign Affairs*, who invited me to turn it into an article. I had never published anything, and I'd certainly never intended to publish this. In fact, the thought hadn't even crossed my mind. On the basis of that article, I was later made executive director of a study group at the Council on Foreign Relations called "Nuclear Weapons and Foreign Policy." This led to a bestselling book and that, in turn, propelled me into a role in contemporary foreign policy. If I'd not had that encounter with Arthur, I may have ended up in the same place in my life, but it would have taken quite a bit longer. Today, whenever Arthur complains about my policy points, I tease him: He's the one who put me here!

BE HONEST

In 1969, when Richard Nixon took office, I was teaching at Harvard University. I had spent twelve years opposing Nixon in campaigns at the side of Nelson Rockefeller, so I really couldn't believe it when Nixon called me and offered me the position of national security advisor. I had never met Nixon, but I was very honest with him. "Mr. President," I said, "I have opposed you all my life, and I'll need to speak with some of my friends to find out whether I can keep their friendship if I go to work for you." He should have told me to get lost. Instead, he said, "Take a week."

I really wasn't sure what to do. I was very close to Nelson Rockefeller, and a few days later, when he came back from his ranch in Venezuela, I told him what happened. He said, "You must be out of your mind! The president-elect is taking a much bigger chance on you than you are on him. Secondly, when the president of the United States asks you to do something, you say yes, unless you have an overwhelming reason to decline." He continued, "Here's a telephone. You call him immediately and say you're accepting without conditions." I took the job—but, as it happened, I lost all my friends, including those from Harvard. I didn't lose them for taking the position; I lost them for carrying out the policies of the president.

OVERCOME YOUR FEELINGS
AND GIVE TO OTHERS

I've learned that you can't use history like a cookbook. You learn as a child that a hot stove burns you, but the knowledge is useless unless you're able to recognize a hot stove. In this sense, you can learn from history. Kraemer gave me a real sense of history, which I hadn't had in such a profound way. Nelson Rockefeller taught me how to operate in the practical world, meaning the world of big organizations and politics. (Of course, he lost every campaign where I worked with him. So my lessons were, in a way, negative—but I learned from them and from him.)

Later on, when I became famous, I was at a lunch at the University Club. Rockefeller's office was right behind the building. There was a big crowd assembled in front of the club, and I was pretty shy. I didn't know how to handle the crowd. I found a side door to his office and said to him, "I really can't handle this." He responded, "Never do this again. People do you the honor of wanting to touch you, or see you, and wave to you, and you owe them that. You overcome your feelings, and you go out there and let them do it."

I have acted on this advice ever since.

JACK LaLANNE

FITNESS EXPERT

★ ★ ★

Despite nine decades on this earth, Jack LaLanne greets every second as if it were the best of his life. He leaps out at you—literally bounces into a room and exudes life! In fact, he claims that what kills a person is inactivity. If that's the case, he'll be alive for many years to come.

While some people celebrate their birthdays with exotic trips or big parties, Jack has had a unique way of celebrating. When he turned forty-one, he swam from Alcatraz to Fisherman's Island in handcuffs. At forty-two he broke a world pushup record. At sixty he repeated the swim from Alcatraz to Fisherman's Island—this time handcuffed, shackled, and towing a thousand-pound boat. At age sixty-five he did the same thing, but towing sixty-five boats hauling sixty-five hundred pounds of wood pulp. At seventy he donned the handcuffs and shackles again, and towed seventy boats—each of them with seventy people on board!

On days when you need a little inspiration, think of Jack.

IF MAN MAKES IT, DON'T EAT IT

When I was fifteen, I would eat only junk food: cake, pies, ice cream, and soda pop. With all that junk and all that sugar, I was destroying the B vitamins in my body. I had no energy. I had splitting headaches every day, and I couldn't participate in sports because I was so sick. I couldn't exercise, I was so weak. I was like an alcoholic, but I was addicted to sugar. I couldn't sleep at night. It was hell on earth. I would have died if I hadn't changed.

Then, one night, my mother took me to a lecture given by a pioneer in nutrition named Paul Bragg. He wasn't as into exercise as he was into good nutrition. But that night he said one thing I've never forgotten: "If man makes it, don't eat it." I went home that night and thought to myself, "Jack, you're not living right. You don't exercise, and you eat food that's bad for you." I asked God to give me the willpower to refrain from eating food that was killing me. I joined the Berkeley YMCA and started exercising. When I changed my eating habits, my life changed immediately.

If something saved your life that way, you'd be enthusiastic about it, too.

STICK TO YOUR GUNS

Very few people at that time realized how important physical activity was. But I was fascinated. I started studying anatomy and the workings of the body, the muscles, and the bones, and then started devising exercises for particular muscle groups. I had my first gym when I was a senior in high school. All the policemen and firemen who couldn't pass their physicals came to see me, and soon I had them working out of my backyard. After two weeks, every one of them passed the physical.

In 1936, I opened America's first gym in downtown Oakland, California. Until then, the only gyms were the ones boxers used to work out in. Everybody thought it was a crazy endeavor. Doctors were telling people that Jack LaLanne was a liar and a cheat. They said, "He's got old people working out. They'll have heart attacks. He's got women lifting weights. They'll start looking like men." All the newspapers started writing about it. Those were the dark ages, I'll tell you. I was a strict vegetarian for six years, and that made it even worse in some people's minds! But I just stuck to my guns. The newspapers said I'd be out of business in six months.

IF PEOPLE DON'T COME TO YOU, GO TO THEM

During those first three months, people would walk back and forth in front of the gym, but no one would come in. Everybody stayed away from me like I was poison because of all the bad press. But one day I was giving a massage and it just popped in my head: "Jack, if people aren't coming to you, you've got to go to them." So that day I put on a tight T-shirt—I had a forty-nine-inch chest and a twenty-eight-inch waist—and I went to the biggest high school in the San Francisco Bay area at noontime. All the kids recognized me and started taunting me. Well, I picked out the fattest kid I could find and the skinniest kid I could find. I got their phone numbers, addresses, and names. I told the parents of the fat boy that I could take ten to fifteen pounds off him, and I told the parents of the skinny boy that I could put twenty-five pounds on him. At night I would go to their homes and work with them. Well, they both accomplished their goals—and after about six months I had so many kids in my gym that I had to cut the membership down. Then the adults started coming.

PRACTICE WHAT YOU PREACH

When I went on television in 1951, the same old thing started again. The press all said, *We'll give him two weeks and then he'll be off the air.* You can't believe the stuff I've gone through, boy. I hear Rev. Billy Graham preach about the life after, but I'm here for the life now. You've got to work for today, for this moment. You're never too old. Even people who are ninety years old can double their strength and double their endurance in six to eight weeks by exercising and eating right. Any stupid dummy can die. Dying is easy: Don't exercise; don't worry about what you eat. Living is a pain in the butt. You've got to train like it's an athletic event. You've got to have goals and challenges. You've got to work out and stretch your muscles. Dying is easy. Living is tough.

IF IT TASTES GOOD, SPIT IT OUT

Today, everyone is talking about exercise, but there are still too many fat people. Those diet books are bad. The authors write books to make a buck. It's ridiculous. They say don't eat carbohydrates or starches. Don't mix fat and starches at all. That's just somebody trying to sell a book, somebody telling a lie. It's no secret that you need to eat four to five raw vegetables a day, five pieces of raw fruit, and eat natural whole grains. If it tastes good, spit it out. You'll never get fat that way.

WORK AT LIVING

I work at living. I've never been more successful than I am today. My lectures are planned a year in advance, and my schedule is jam-packed. There's no doubt that your attitude toward life is important. I'm so enthusiastic about the information I tell people, because I figure I could save somebody's life. I'm here to help people, and they know it. You gotta think, "What is the food that I put in my mouth doing to the most important person on this earth?" That's you. God helps those who help themselves. You have to do it for yourself. God gives you the power, but you have to use that power. If anything happens to Jack LaLanne, good or bad, I made it happen.

YOU'RE HALF DEAD.
YOU'VE GOTTA START LIVING

This is the stuff they should be teaching kids in grammar school. Think of all the medications doctors prescribe for kids to make them feel better. These kids eat crap. You wouldn't give your dog a cup of coffee and a doughnut, yet that's how a lot of people wake up and start their day. They wonder why they're sick, why they're tired. I just bought a new Mercedes convertible. Would I put water in the gas tank? Of course not. How about your human machine? You fill it with man-made ice cream, cakes, muffins, soda pop. Did you ever read the label on a can of food? You can't pronounce half the ingredients. It's filled with preservatives, with artificial flavors and colors. That food's been killed and cooked.

When I give lectures, I have one thing to offer to help somebody live longer and better—my mind. You gotta wake up! You're half dead. You gotta start living.

IF I HADN'T STARTED EXERCISING,
I WOULDN'T BE HERE TODAY

Though it was my mother who took me to that health lecture long ago, she didn't know anything about nutrition. By the time I became interested in physical fitness, she was in a sanitarium suffering from a nervous breakdown. Once she was released from the sanitarium, I got her exercising and eating right. She became healthy again. I tried to get my dad to exercise and change the food he ate, but he didn't listen to me. He died of a heart attack at age fifty. If I hadn't started exercising and eating right, I absolutely wouldn't be here today. I was fortunate. I found the truth at an early age.

JOHN LEHMAN

**FORMER SECRETARY OF THE
UNITED STATES NAVY**

★ ★ ★

John Lehman is a very cool guy. He says what he thinks, which can be a very dangerous habit in politics. There's nothing more frustrating than asking someone about the growth of Islamic fundamentalism and its impact on America and having them dance around the topic for fear of stepping on toes. I get the feeling people wear steel-toed boots around John Lehman!

While we are at war, Lehman says, it is not a war on terrorism, but a war against violent, Islamic fundamentalism. Terrorism, he says, is merely a tool— like kamikaze tactics. When discussing September 11, he places some of the blame on our own government, including himself. He vividly recalls when the Marine barracks were bombed in Beirut and our military did nothing to retaliate. He believes that this gave ideas to Osama bin Laden. The government of Iran was behind those murders, so many people continued to believe that terrorism was state-sponsored. No one was prepared for non-state-sponsored terrorism. Even now, he cites how little is being done to counter extremist schools that are teaching and preaching jihad against America.

I had always wondered what pulled John Lehman into politics. When I asked him, his answer was true to form: Our government was so screwed up, he said, he knew he could do better!

MONEY SHOULDN'T BE THE BOTTOM LINE

I greatly admired my father, who was the skipper of an LCS ship in the Pacific during World War II. He really loved the navy. He didn't push me into the navy; I just grew up wanting to be like him. I talked to him about my career plans, and whether or not I should go to business school, because I had been admitted to the M.B.A. program at Wharton. While I was flattered to have been accepted there, I was fascinated by national security policy, and really wanted to get a Ph.D. in foreign policy. My father, who was by then a businessman, would have probably preferred for me to get the M.B.A., but this is what he said: "In the final analysis, you should follow your instinct. Because you're the only one who knows what that is. Don't choose based on what other people want you to do. Follow your gut. If you love what you're doing, money shouldn't be the bottom line."

The older I get, the more I realize just how sound that advice was. So I ended up getting my doctorate. But here's the funny part: Even after he encouraged me to do what I loved, when I went for the Ph.D., he asked, "How the hell are you going to make a living with a Ph.D?" I couldn't answer that!

EXPRESS YOURSELF THROUGH WRITING

I had a great-uncle named George Kelly, a Pulitzer Prize–winning author who lived in Hollywood and New York and wrote and directed many Broadway plays. He moved to Philadelphia when I was in high school and became hugely influential in my life. I spent a lot of time with him, having dinner and lunch together. He'd talk and talk, and I loved listening to him; he had such a beautiful command of the English language, he was captivating. He encouraged me to write and I began to show him essays. He'd correct my English style and offer guidance in my writing. That early guidance motivated me to write books, and I've written about six or seven of them so far. By the way, he was also Grace Kelly's uncle. Grace's father, Jack, and my grandmother were brother and sister. It was through our Uncle George that Grace and I became close, despite our age difference. Uncle George motivated her to pursue a career in the theater. In fact, her first role was in the Bucks County Theatre summer stock's production of Uncle George's play *The Torch Bearers,* which got critical notice in New York City. Uncle George was a very influential character. He taught me how to express myself through writing, and this skill has certainly helped me articulate the policy positions I've been so involved in promoting during my career in government.

DON'T WANT POWER, WANT CHANGE

Two people motivated me to go into government and focus on national security and defense. First was Jim Dockerty, who was head of the international relations department at St. Joseph's University, where I earned my bachelor of science degree. The second—from the University of Pennsylvania, where I earned my doctorate—was the great Robert Strausz-Hupe, who was the founder of the Foreign Policy Research Institute. Both were very charismatic figures who were very influential in the policy world. Their advice about working in foreign policy was, "Don't want to go into government to have a powerful job; go in to change things." Through their example, I realized that the job you took was irrelevant if it enabled you to correct important mistakes and change the inefficiencies inherent in government. The culture there wasn't focused on the endgame of planning to be secretary of state or secretary of defense. It was all about the belief that there was no limit to what you could do in Washington if you were really passionate and did the intellectual homework.

Ronald Reagan had different words for the same insight. There is no limit to the good a person can do, he said, if he doesn't care who gets the credit. Both Dockerty and Strausz-Hupe had done some government service, but they weren't interested in the perks or the power; they were interested in the policy. Having been in the government on and off since 1969, I can categorize every single person I've met in government as being one or the other: motivated by ego, or by a passion to improve the policy.

IF YOU KNOW YOU'RE RIGHT, ACT ON IT

I was fortunate to be among a group of intellectuals at Penn and St. Joseph's who were deeply committed to our country. They had all served in World War II and had been advisers to Republicans and Democrats during the Cold War. It was through them that I first met Henry Kissinger and Richard Allen. It was Richard Allen who hired me into the Nixon administration to work on the National Security Council.

My formative years were during the Johnson presidency, when the country had gotten so far off course. It was already being screwed up in the later Eisenhower years, and the Johnson years only made things worse, although the Kennedy years were kind of cool. Still, when I graduated from college in 1964, I really felt the country was in a mess. The assumptions that were being made, and the policies being carried out, were just wrong, and I could hardly wait to get involved. I thought to myself, "I know I can do better than that." It may sound arrogant, but I didn't think it was arrogant at the time—and even now I don't, because I still think I was right.

VALUE WELL-MEANING COUNSEL

My father used to joke and say, "Here's my son, the professional student. Don't ask him how he's going to make a living because he doesn't know." For him, a member of the World War II generation, the smart thing to do was to join a company and stay with that company. Everyone had a career path. I had no idea what my career path would be, but I knew I wanted to be involved in changing policy.

Despite his jokes, I deeply valued the counsel I received from my father. I never told him exactly how much his counsel helped me, but I hope he knew it. One time, while I was secretary of the navy, I was the marshal of the Fourth of July parade in Philadelphia. At the parade, a journalist asked my father, "Your son is the youngest navy secretary ever. Did you ever think he'd be secretary of the navy when he was growing up in Glenside?" My father said, "Never in a million years." But of course he was very supportive of everything I did. When I earned my degrees from St. Joe's, Penn, and Cambridge University, he said, "That's all great, and you absolutely should do it. But someday you're going to have to think about what you're going to do for a living." Well, I did figure it out, and I've been successful in business at Sperry Marine, PaineWebber, and, of course, my own firm, J.F. Lehman & Company. But in my heart it has always been my work in government policy that has been most rewarding.

JUSTIN McBRIDE

Imagine climbing on top of a 1,700-pound beast with no saddle—just a piece of rope to hang onto! That's what Justin McBride does when he goes to work. The moment the bucking chute opens, Justin's pay is determined by the bull he's riding. The more speed, power, direction changes, and body rolls, the better the bull and the tougher the ride. Justin's got to stay on for eight seconds, all the while displaying constant control, good body position, and a little spurring (which gets extra style points). Oh, and he has to do all this one-handed, and gets disqualified if his other hand touches his body or the bull.

Few make it. Justin McBride makes it look easy.

TRY YOUR HARDEST, AND YOU'LL SLEEP WELL THAT NIGHT

It was clear from a pretty young age that I was going to be a bull rider. I was about three when I climbed on my first calf! Early on, I got some great advice from my dad. It became the tenet for how I live my life and how I approach my job. "If you try your hardest," Dad told me, "you may not win every time. But you'll sleep well that night."

PUT IT ALL OUT ON THE TABLE

Every day, when I go out there and climb into that chute, I start with the attitude that I've got to win. Then I go all out, until there's nothing left. Some days I don't make it to the eight-second bell; if I make a fundamental mistake, I just get beat. I can live with that. If I know that I gave it everything, that it's all out on the table and there's nothing left in me, then win or lose, at least I can fall asleep that night. There's nothing worse than going back to your room and thinking about what you could have done right if you'd just tried a little harder. That makes a loss real tough to accept.

When I follow my dad's advice, I sleep well.

John Mack (second from left) *and his family*

JOHN MACK

BUSINESSMAN

John Mack is extremely loyal to his supporters and ruthless to people who stand in his way—hence the moniker "Mack the Knife." His leadership ability, charisma, and character are such that people are devoted to him and will follow him, despite any controversy or risk, because they believe in him. He has the ability to sense future trends and convince those around him to move forward with him to implement his vision.

Most people on Wall Street think John is tough, hard-nosed, and driven. But those who have worked closely with him note his loyalty, kindness, and generosity. Behind the scenes, people turn to John for help and counsel. He treats friends as he would treat his own family. John began working as a bond salesman for Morgan Stanley in 1972, and rose to become president of the company twenty-one years later. In 1997, after the company merged with brokerage and credit card giant Dean Witter, Discover & Co., he became CEO. In 2001, he quit and moved to Credit Suisse Group as co-chief executive. When his strategy clashed with the bank's leadership, he left. John is now chairman of the hedge fund company Pequot Capital Management Inc.

MAINTAIN YOUR REPUTATION

My father, mother, and uncle were old-fashioned immigrants who believed in three things: religion, education, and reputation. Growing up, I learned that you had to do whatever it took to maintain your reputation. This idea really stuck with me, and even today I'm proud that people tell me, "You've got a great reputation for integrity and honesty." I have tried to follow in my father's and my uncle's footsteps. They were up at 5:30 every day. They each owned their own business, and if they borrowed money from the bank, it always got paid back.

My parents made sure that we were all involved in church and community service. Every Christmas my father would raise money for orphanages.
He didn't do this because he had any connection to those orphans; rather, he
simply believed that any institution that would take in kids and help them
was a good cause.

PAY YOUR DEBTS

My father used to lend money to other immigrants, and it was always interesting to see who would pay him back and who would not. It was a working
example of how you needed to preserve your reputation. My father would
appeal to those who weren't paying their debts under the guise that he used
this money as a multiplier. He explained that when he got that money back
he could then lend to someone else. He told them that there was an obligation to pay because he'd accepted the task of helping them. In some cases,
he'd get the money; other times he wouldn't. Hearing my family and others
talk about those who didn't pay their debts had a searing impact on me. I
knew I wanted to be a man people could always trust.

GIVE BACK TO THE COMMUNITY

In college I told my parents, "I am who I am because of you." I remember
the conversation very specifically, because I was very emotional about it. I
wanted to make sure they knew I appreciated them.

My father passed away while I was in college. He never got the chance
to see me succeed in business. My mother did see it, and I know she was
very pleased and happy. The family is so proud of what I've accomplished
in business, but they're happier about the fact that my wife, Christy, and I
have given back quite a bit to the community—not just money, but our
time as well. We support Duke University with scholarships. If you go to
my hometown, there are probably just a handful of families who could afford to send their child to Duke or any other top-flight private university.
So we supply scholarships specifically for high school graduates from my

hometown. We have never had anything named after ourselves, but there is a small civic center in my town where the senior citizens, the Kiwanis Club, and other groups meet. They want to expand it, and we've given money for the project.

We've asked them to name the building after my father.

MEL MARTINEZ

UNITED STATES SENATOR

Mel Martinez is the first Cuban American to win a U.S. Senate seat. And if it weren't for Peter Pan, he wouldn't even be here. Operation Peter Pan was a Roman Catholic humanitarian effort that brought fourteen thousand children from Cuba to the United States in the early 1960s.

What influenced his rise from refugee status to one of the most prominent positions in the country? His father's incessant reminder that even in a communist country, education is an asset no one can take away. That advice has made all the difference for Mel.

LEARN THE CULTURE FIRST

I was six years old when I escaped from Cuba. I came alone because my whole family couldn't escape at the same time. I went through a very difficult time in those first weeks and months. I was lonely and confused. "What am I doing here?" I wondered. "How am I ever going to make it? When will I see my family again?"

It was very, very difficult to overcome those fears. But I was cared for by the Catholic Church and put into a foster home. I started going to school even before I could speak English well. It was a great opportunity for all my classmates to make fun of me. I got teased a lot. But I started playing sports with them, and the ball field is a great equalizer. It was a door opener for me; it allowed me to become one of the gang. When I walked out of the classroom onto the ball field and hit a line drive, the kids decided they could understand my broken English a little better! Soon enough, the kids were treating me like I was normal, and I began to feel normal, and that was a huge breakthrough.

As an immigrant, I believe that it's more important to learn the culture than it is to learn the language, at least at first. As a child I didn't understand the American culture. My vision of America was what I saw in the movies—either cowboy movies or gang movies about New York. I thought every street corner had either a guy on a horse or a kid with a switchblade. Once I came to learn about the culture and the people, though, the language came more easily—and I became part of the society.

NO ONE CAN TAKE AWAY YOUR KNOWLEDGE

Before I came to America, my father constantly talked to me about education. The one thing the Communists and Castro couldn't take away from people, he said, was their education. That left me with a really strong message about the importance of education and how it can change a person's life.

My foster care officially ended when I was eighteen, but my foster family said that I could live with them even though they were no longer receiving any financial assistance. I began to work part-time jobs, sometimes two of them at a time. I would work summer construction jobs and anything else I could get my hands on, just so I could continue going to school. I went to a junior college in Orlando, Florida. In my second year of college, my parents finally arrived from Cuba. They lost everything they had worked for all their lives. All of the personal possessions that seemed so important at the time—the family home, the car, the furniture—were gone.

Dad was right: The only thing they were left with was their knowledge.

YOU'VE GOT TO KEEP ON LEARNING

By the time they arrived I'd saved up two hundred dollars, and we all went out and spent it on a used '59 Chevrolet, and we were a proud bunch. I helped my family settle into America; I even took my dad for his driver's license. All of a sudden, the world was upside down: I was a nineteen-year-old kid and I was parenting my parents. I taught them how to shop at the grocery store, how to use the Laundromat, even helped dad find a job. Eventually, they made their new life in America. I transferred to Florida State, got my undergraduate degree, and went to law school after that.

No matter what I accomplished, my father would always say, "You haven't done enough. You've got to keep on learning." I would have been content to go to work, but my dad had other ideas. He really didn't care what career I chose; he just wanted me to get as much education as I could. That encouraged me; it drove me to go to law school, which opened so many doors in my life. Often, immigrant families are obliged to send their children to work as soon as they can, but my dad had his priorities right when he encouraged me to pursue higher education.

SACRIFICE NOW FOR A LARGER GOAL LATER

Because my dad and I weren't together while I was growing up, I never went through the rebellious teenage stage. I cherished the advice he'd given me as a young boy, and I always remained pretty impressed with whatever he had to say to me. Young people must realize they need to sacrifice now for a larger goal later, because when they reach it the dividends can be wonderful.

This is a country of wonderful opportunity. If you have an education, you're on an even playing field—no matter who you are.

MARY MEEKER

FINANCIAL ANALYST

★ ★ ★

When few people even knew what tech companies actually did, Mary Meeker, a managing director at Morgan Stanley, was urging them to buy stock in little-known companies like Microsoft, Compaq, and Dell. She realized how the Internet was going to change the world. She also realized that companies could exploit the Internet to grow, diversify, and broaden their customer base faster than they'd ever been able to do in the past. Companies that continued to come up with new technology—or novel ways to use the Internet to create buyers or sellers, like eBay or Amazon.com—were the wave of the future. People who followed her advice from the start were handsomely rewarded.

LEARN, EARN, AND SERVE

In the early 1980s, I had just graduated from college and was working in a junior position at Merrill Lynch in Chicago. John Shad had recently been named chair of the U.S. Securities and Exchange Commission. A pal of mine from high school, who was working in Washington, D.C., invited me to a small meeting hosted by Shad. The topic under discussion was the financial services industry, but the one thing I remember about the meeting was something that John said.

John said that he had chosen to dedicate the first third of his career to getting an education. The second third he devoted to making a living. And the final third he would spend giving back. Years later, I learned that John had shared this approach with many people in his life—so much so that it came to be known as "John Shad's learn, earn, and serve philosophy."

Even at that moment, as I was just beginning my career, John's philosophy struck a chord. I decided to structure my career the same way.

Senator Zell Miller and his mother, Birdie, 1944

ZELL MILLER

UNITED STATES SENATOR

★ ★ ★

Depending on whom you speak with, you can get some very diverse and heated re-
actions to Senator Zell Miller. I recall listening to Senator Miller in 1992 when
he delivered the keynote address on behalf of Bill Clinton. I liked what he said.
Then, in 2004, at the same venue—Madison Square Garden in New York
City—I heard him deliver the keynote address on behalf of George W. Bush.
Again, I liked what he said. His style combines Texas-style stump speeches with
spitball rhetoric. I grinned at the spitball lines he threw . . . and I still do today.

Where do they make men like Zell Miller? In Georgia, and in the marines!
I'm one of those folks who likes politicians who drop the party tag and call it like
they see it. I love Zell. He governed Georgia from the centrist Democrat play-
book. He was tough on crime and reformed welfare. President Bill Clinton called
him "brilliant." Today, some Democrats call him "crazy." If he is, I'm in his
loony bin.

IF YOU WANT DESSERT, EAT YOUR SPINACH

My father died when I was a couple of weeks old, so my mother raised both
my sister and me on her own. We grew up in a remote little valley in Appalachia. From my earliest days, my mother said, "Take what you want,
sayeth the Lord—take it and pay for it." I was a grown man before I realized
that's not in the Bible. It was just my mother's scripture. She meant that
there was always a price to pay for anything in life, and that you have to
work for what you really want. I don't think there's any more fundamental
truth out there. It has been a guiding principle of my life. I say it to my children and to my grandchildren.

I think it's particularly important today, because a lot of people—
especially young people—seem to want everything given to them. They

want something for nothing. They want dessert, but they're not willing to eat the spinach to get it. If I want to write a book, I have to labor and pay the price for it. Somewhere in the Bible it says that the fruits of labor come only to those who labor for the fruits. Well, that was what my mother was saying. And it was the best advice I've ever gotten.

GET BACK UP AND KEEP TRYING

In my political career, I was defeated three times. I've won a lot of elections, but I was defeated early on. I ran for Congress twice and for the Senate once, and all three times I was defeated. Anybody with any sense would have figured after that third defeat that "Hey, they don't want you in office!" I kept thinking, "No, I've got something to offer." So I kept running. If you look at toddlers, you realize that's how they learn to walk. They can't understand it when you tell them to stand up. There's just something inside them that makes them want to get up on their feet. And then, when they take a step, they fall down the first few times. There's something in them, though, that makes them get back up and keep trying, and finally they can walk over to the couch or to their mama's arms. I think that's the way it is in life.

YOU WANT SOMETHING, WORK FOR IT

I've always thought that the GI Bill, back after World War II, was the best government program I ever heard of. It was built on the idea that if you give your service to the nation, you get to go to college. I went to college on the GI Bill.

One of the best things to come along recently—and even those who opposed it back in the 1990s would agree today—was the welfare reform legislation that enabled recipients to get off welfare. The government will help those in need, but it won't continue to give you aid forever. I think that policy was really one of the things that made me become such a big supporter of Bill Clinton when he was running for president back in 1992. His welfare policy reflected the kind of life philosophy that I believe in. Unfortunately, he got away from that in a lot of ways, and it was the Republicans who ended up passing the reform in Congress. Either way, it was one of the best things that he did.

FORGET THE CEREMONY AND REMEMBER THE SUBSTANCE

My mom lived to see me elected lieutenant governor, but not to go to the Senate. The day I was qualified to run for lieutenant governor, I wanted her there in Atlanta with me. I called her and said, "I wish you'd be down here with me when I qualify to run statewide for lieutenant governor." And she said, "Well, I can't. I'm too busy." If you knew my mother, she was always busy. She never sat down. So I accepted what she said, but I got to thinking about it overnight. I called her up the next day and I said, "Why don't you come down here and be with me? I'm about to take a major step, and I just want you with me." And she said, "I don't have time. I'm too busy." And I shot back at her, "Well, what are you too busy doing?" And she said, "I'm building a sign in my front yard that says VOTE FOR ZELL MILLER FOR LIEU-TENANT GOVERNOR." She didn't have time for all that ceremonial stuff be-cause she was busy doing the important grassroots campaign instead.

JOIN THE MARINES. WE MAKE MEN

I grew up in a home without a father, and I missed that support. I wasn't a perfect kid, and I got into all kinds of trouble. Finally, I joined the Marine Corps. The reason I did was that I had wrecked a car. I was drinking moon-shine liquor, and I ran my car into a ditch. They took me to jail. I got to thinking about all the lessons that my mother had tried to teach me, and I re-membered a sign that said, JOIN THE MARINES. WE MAKE MEN. And I thought I needed to be made into a man so I joined the Marine Corps.

They picked up where she left off.

Ray Charles and Ronnie Milsap

RONNIE MILSAP

COUNTRY AND ROCK MUSICIAN

★ ★ ★

It is rare to find someone as accomplished in the music industry as Ronnie Mil-sap. He's had number one hits on the soul, pop, and country charts. I loved his music before I knew anything about him as a person. I recall cruising to school with the top down in my VW bug listening to his songs and singing along at the top of my lungs . . . very out of key!

Ronnie had a string of six number one hits in 1976 alone, and another ten consecutive number ones between 1980 and 1982. Today, forty-one number one songs and one Grammy nomination later, he is a legend. Ronnie feels he's been blessed his entire life, although he has overcome huge obstacles. Ronnie was born blind, which his mother interpreted as a punishment from God. She and Ron-nie's father divorced, and he was given to his grandparents. They soon sent him away to a school for the blind. But within a year he was declared a violin virtu-oso, and his gift for music was recognized by all.

REACH FOR THE STARS, WORK FOR THE SKILLS

My life began to change at the Governor Morehead School for the Blind in Raleigh, North Carolina. The school had incredible teachers, small classes, and a wonderful music department where I studied classical music for ten years. The teachers instilled in us the will to go out and reach for the stars. They also taught me very early on that if I was going to function in a society as a blind individual, I needed to have the right skills.

I talk to a lot of children today who don't read Braille. I'm very disappointed that only about 11 percent of the blind population reads Braille. The kids say they don't need to read Braille because now they can scan everything into a computer, which will read it aloud to them. But Braille is one of the skills necessary to live as a blind person. Braille was the first thing I learned. Ninety percent of all working blind people read Braille.

In school, from the age of six, I had a violin teacher named Wallace Grieves. He was a wonderful violinist, and he's the reason I worked so hard to learn the basic skills of music. I wanted to please him so much that I practiced constantly, so that I could play in the school orchestra with him. As a result, when I left Governor Morehead School for the Blind to go to college, I had the skills I needed. I could play violin, guitar, and woodwind instruments and was a classically trained pianist.

WORK UNTIL YOU GET
WHAT YOUR HEART WANTS

I went on to Young Harris Junior College in Georgia and there I met the person who gave me my inspiration.

For the first couple of days in college, I thought, "Well, that's great. I'm the only blind person in this college." But because I was skilled, I was able to deal with it. I could sit down and play piano, and that helped me discover that music breaks the barriers. It breaks the ice, and all of a sudden everybody wants to talk to you. Music connects everyone that way.

It was in college that I connected with a political science teacher named Zell Miller, whom I'm friends with to this day. He made me feel that I could do anything. He told me, "If you've got your heart set on something, work until you get it." That's what I saw him do. To this day, I look at what he's accomplished in his life, and the first thought that crosses my mind is that he is a brave man. He has the same charisma now that he had forty years ago. I never told Zell in so many words what an inspiration he was in my life, but I do brag about him. I played for one of his fund-raisers when he was running for governor down there in Georgia. Who would have thought that our paths would keep crossing? It's an interesting journey, and you never know how it's going to play out. Knowing Zell has been one of the high points in my life. It was from my high regard for him that I embarked on an academic career.

FOLLOW WHERE YOUR HEART
TELLS YOU TO GO

I'd been accepted into law school at Emory in Atlanta when I met Ray Charles in 1963. I was at a concert to see Ray and Little Stevie Wonder, who was just thirteen. At the concert I wanted to go backstage to meet Ray, but the people at the door said, "No, that's forbidden." But I just kept saying, "I really want to go and meet him!" and his pilot overheard and said, "Come on back." So I went back to Ray's dressing room. Ray came in, and there were a lot of people around him, but he took time to talk to me. I said, "I play music." There was a piano in the dressing room, and so I started to play for them. I had a lot of courage, because I was young and I didn't even think to worry about what people thought of me. I just played.

I told Ray I was about to go to law school. He said, "Well, you can be a lawyer if you want to, son, but there's a lot of music in your heart. If I were you, I'd follow where my heart tells me to go." That made a big impression on me. Later on, in 2003, I played with Ray at one of his last concerts, in Houston, Texas. I spent the day with him, and I knew he wasn't feeling well, but I didn't realize just how sick he really was. He would always say to me, "Ronald, let's get our agents together and do some shows together in Las Vegas." We played TV shows over the years and played for presidents. He was my greatest musical influence, but he was also a real friend. And I'll always remember thinking, if Ray Charles thinks I can make it in music, I want to make it in music.

SEE YOUR CHANCE, AND TAKE IT

Of course, once I declined my scholarship to Emory, which was being paid for by the state of North Carolina, I was told, "If you go into music, you'll wind up out on the street and a liability to the states. You need to finish school and get a real job, see, to have a substantial life." But I saw my chance in music, and I decided to take it. It was 1964, and I also met my wife, Joyce, around the same time. We've been married thirty-nine years and she's been a guiding light for me. She's kept my feet on the ground, but encouraged me to do everything I want to do.

PASS IT ON

When I got to Nashville, my biggest inspiration was Charley Pride. I'd been doing rock 'n' roll in Memphis and played on a couple of albums with Elvis, Isaac Hayes, and Booker T. Jones. Good stuff. I came to Nashville as a last resort, and figured that if I couldn't make it there, I probably would need to go back to law school. I called around and made the appointments. Luckily, I got to see Jack Johnson, who was Charley Pride's manager. I was playing the King of the Road Hotel, and Jack came and heard me. Three days later, he had me in his office and I signed a management contract. Charley Pride had me on his TV show, and I learned from observing how he dealt with people and how kind he was to the fans. I had never had that level of success before, so it was totally new to me.

After I'd had three or four number one records, Charley came to me one day and said, "You need to go out and do your own shows. You can do a whole lot better going off and doing your own show." So I said, "You're right, and I can't tell you how much I appreciate what you've done for me, Charley." And his parting words were, "Just pass it on." It was great advice, because we all run into the younger artists coming into Nashville. I watched Charley conduct himself with style and dignity and class. That's the Charley Pride I know. He taught me that you need to be available to pass it on to the ones who are interested enough to want to learn.

ANNE MULCAHY

CHAIRMAN AND CEO, XEROX

Soon after graduating from Marymount College in Tarrytown, New York, Anne Mulcahy began working as a field representative for Xerox. Over the years she grew with the company, eventually becoming vice president for human relations, where she oversaw management development and employee training. In 2000, just as the company was facing severe financial problems, she became the company's CEO. Within three years, she had turned the business around.

Anne's style, colleagues say, is basic nuts-and-bolts; it's goal-oriented and based on common sense. Plus, in a field where many women try to "out-macho" men to prove themselves, Anne Mulcahy made it to the top without changing who she is.

FIRST, GET THE COW OUT OF THE DITCH

The best advice I've ever received didn't come from a leadership guru or a business book. It came from a customer who saw our situation more clearly than most others. About four years ago, I was hosting a breakfast meeting with some of our customers in Dallas. One of them was both a prominent businessman and a real mover and shaker in the civic and political world of Dallas: Albert Black, the owner of a company called On-Target Supplies and Logistics.

Albert told me that I reminded him of the farmer whose cow got stuck in the ditch. "You've got to do three things," he said. "First, get the cow out of the ditch. Second, find out how the cow got in the ditch. Third, make sure you do whatever it takes so the cow doesn't go in the ditch again." This is the best advice I've ever been given, and I've lived by it ever since.

FOCUS ON THE FUNDAMENTALS

When thinking about our business and the challenges we face, I like to focus on the fundamentals, maintain a rational view of problems, and understand how our operations work. In fact, Albert Black's cow story has become a bit of a catchphrase with some of the Xerox leadership team. No one ever likes to be responsible for a cow's going in the ditch, but we all work together to get it out.

Colonel Oliver North (right) *and Brigadier General John Grinalds*

OLIVER NORTH

RETIRED LIEUTENANT COLONEL, UNITED STATES MARINE CORPS

*To the men and women of the United States military, Ollie North is a rock star.
They believe him, trust him, and many would lay down their lives for him.
Why? Because they know he'd do the same for them.*

*If you spend one minute speaking with Ollie, you will never doubt his dedication to America. This is a man who sincerely and completely loves his country.
In twenty-two years as a marine, he was awarded the Silver Star, the Bronze
Star for valor, and two purple hearts for wounds in combat. He coordinated the
invasion of Granada and the attempt to arrest the hijackers of the* Achille
Lauro. *He is also known for his involvement in the Iran-Contra affair, which
sold weapons to Iran to fund rebels fighting the Marxist government in
Nicaragua. But it is important to note that the convictions against North were
overturned in 1990.*

I often speak with Ollie while he's traveling with a battalion in Iraq. Although he's retired from the military, his life's goal remains the same: to do anything, in any way, at any time, to better serve and protect America.

COME TO KNOW YOUR LORD AND SAVIOR

In 1978, I was thirty-five years old, working as the Operations Officer for a
U.S. Marine Battalion Landing Team, and I finally listened to some advice
that changed my life. Our unit was about to deploy for six months to the
Mediterranean and the Battalion Commander, Lieutenant Colonel John Grinalds, slapped me on the chest with a copy of the Good Book and said, "Major, you need to read this so that you come to know your Lord and Savior."

I'd grown up in a good, God-fearing, *Leave It to Beaver* kind of 1950s
family. We went to church every Sunday and were basically considered
proper people. My mom and dad had certainly given me plenty of good ad-

vice over the years, but I ignored much of it, being a strong-willed young man. Looking back now, it's pretty clear John Grinalds was able to get through to me in ways that my parents and others couldn't. I realize that's what happens with a lot of us: We often get good advice from others, but sometimes we just don't act on it.

IT'S NOT JUST ABOUT YOU

Taking advice from John Grinalds seemed like the right thing to do. He was not only my commanding officer, he was also a West Point graduate, had been a Rhodes Scholar, a White House Fellow, and everyone knew that someday he was going to be a general. When he asked me to take the assignment as his operations officer, I figured if I hitched my wagon to his rising star, I could go along for the ride.

Before John Grinalds gave me that Holy Bible and told me to read it, I was fairly convinced that I was God's gift to the Marine Corps and my marriage. I was one of those guys who thought it was always all about me. My perfect wife and my three perfect children were there to complement my perfect military career. A self-made man, I'd had all the right assignments, could max any test, had served well in combat, been promoted early, and had a chest full of medals to prove what a great marine I was. Of course officers always get more medals than they deserve, and the troops we lead rarely get the recognition they earn. But that was something I could never have acknowledged before taking John Grinalds's advice. Back then, my ego was so big that I simply couldn't comprehend that I had been doing all the right things for all the wrong reasons.

RISK EVERYTHING TO HUMBLY SERVE

At the time, taking John Grinalds's advice seemed like a fairly simple task; it certainly didn't seem to be a life-changing assignment. All I had to do, I thought, was read the book from cover to cover, so I started with Genesis and read through the stories I'd heard since my youth. But when I got to the eighth chapter of Matthew's Gospel, his description of an unnamed Roman army centurion in Capernaum struck home. Here was a fellow infantry officer putting himself at grave personal peril, risking the equivalent of a court martial by asking Jesus to heal his servant. The centurion doesn't act to further his own career, get a promotion, or advance himself; rather, he does it for a person who would be regarded in those days as insignificant. And, in doing so, this Roman officer acknowledges the authority of Jesus and has the humility to describe himself as unworthy.

Those few verses of scripture hit me like a bullet in the chest. Through my studies of military history I knew that this officer, commanding a remote military garrison in a hostile country, was very likely on the fast track for advancement in the Roman army. Yet he was willing to risk everything by humbly approaching Jesus—all for a servant! And then, after telling the centurion that his servant has been healed, Christ tells his disciples that the Roman soldier has greater faith than anyone else he had yet met in his ministry. It still makes me wonder what Peter and the other eleven thought of *that* pronouncement. They've worn out their sandals walking all over Galilee with Jesus, and here he is telling *them* that their faith wasn't as strong as that of a foreign soldier.

MY INSPIRATION IN ADVERSITY

Reading those words made me realize that the faith, humility, and self-sacrifice embodied in that centurion were the very qualities that made John Grinalds such a remarkable and admirable man. Though he had been highly decorated for valor, he wasn't macho in a conventional sense. Though an intellectual, he didn't belittle those who weren't up to his abilities. By the time we returned to the United States, six months later, I had come to understand what John Grinalds meant by coming to know Jesus Christ as my Lord and Savior. And it really was a life-changing experience. It changed my perception of who I was, what I was here to do, how to do it, where I was going— and why I was going there.

Since then, rarely a day goes by that I fail to spend at least a few minutes reading from my Bible. It is the only book I've ever read from cover to cover more than once. It is my inspiration in adversity, my admonition against discouragement, and my essential preparation for combat—on real battlefields like those I cover for Fox News, and in the day-to-day battles that confront us all.

DRAW ON A SMALL CIRCLE OF FRIENDS

Some of what I've found in the Bible is painful. Some of it can make you smile, but if you're not careful, some of it can make you cry. And it's all made me a more humble man, and hopefully a better husband, father, leader, broadcaster, and friend. The inspiration and encouragement I received from the Book helped me and my family to weather the great controversy in the 1980s known as the Iran-Contra Affair. The Bible gave us faith that all would end well. And, in the end, it did.

The Book has helped me to use my God-given gifts and talents to honor Him. Its pages taught me that I need to have a small circle of friends who can admonish me when I need it and offer a pat on the back when it's deserved. The words reshaped my priorities and my perspective. There was a time in my life when, with my fiery temper, I could take vulgar language to the level of a new art form. That just doesn't happen anymore. It's a small example, but typical of what's happened in my life since I took a fellow marine's advice.

SEMPER FIDELIS

President Bush once said that coming to know Jesus Christ changed his heart and changed his life. I couldn't put it better than that. It's exactly what happened to me and I will be forever grateful to John Grinalds for the Book he gave me and for his order to read it. It was great advice from a man who *lived* the motto of the U.S. Marines: *Semper Fidelis*: Always Faithful.

TED NUGENT

ROCK STAR

Guitar wildman Ted Nugent seems to revel in being the center of controversy. He's the most famous dichotomy in rock: a bona fide arena-rock idol and a life-long antidrug and antialcohol family man. Ted lives both sides to the hilt. He is the six-string master whose classic "Cat Scratch Fever" and many other rock an-thems make him one of rock's top live acts. Anyone who went to one of his 1970s concerts remembers him swinging out onto the stage dressed only in a loincloth and boots or engaging in one of his famous "guitar duels."

But the Nuge is also a dedicated family man who cherishes time hunting and camping with his children. His pro-gun advocacy, position on the NRA's board of directors, and number one–rated conservative radio talk show often clash in people's minds with his long-hair hippie appearance. Ted and his wife, Shemane, also run kids' camps, outdoor education programs, and published Kill It and Grill It, *a cookbook.*

Whenever I talk with Nuge, I'm exhausted afterward: He's so high energy, it's impossible to keep up. He leaves you in the dust. As Ted says, he's on an "uninhib-ited primal scream celebration of sheer defiance and over-the-top irreverent fun."

BUILD ANYWAY

The message I've gotten from all the people I admire in life over my fifty-six greasy rhythm-and-blues years has been, "Be the best that you can be." In fact, there's a great poem called "Anyway" that I try to incorporate into all of my writings now. It reads, in part: "Sometimes you spend your life building a house and someone comes along and burns it down. Build any-way." I conduct my life based on the approach that sometimes you may give the world the best you've got, and still get kicked in the teeth. You should give the world the best you've got anyway. That's how my siblings and I were raised; I got that from the discipline that my dad, a military guy, forced on us. I mean forced in a loving, responsible parental fashion. My mother balanced out his discipline with her humor and joy and her motherliness. I got the best of both worlds—although I didn't always realize this while my dad was raising me, because I was angry that he was such a disciplinarian.

FEAR AND DISCIPLINE

What is life without discipline? Fear was a good motivator for me growing up. Fear of punishment is good enough until you become a thoughtful, reasoning individual at around the age of seven or so. I feared punishment, and that kept me in check until around 1959 or 1960—during the Dobie Gillis time, when the Beatniks were starting to offer me dope and drugs. Because of my discipline, I was already strong enough to turn down even a cigarette. I didn't even know what a marijuana cigarette was, but I knew that these people were conducting themselves in a sloppy, irresponsible, puking, dying, stupid kind of way. At that time, I was performing at sock hops, dances, pool parties, and fraternity parties. My discipline fortified me to withstand what would turn into an avalanche of peer pressure. People wanted me to take booze, tobacco, dope, and drugs. Although I didn't even know what any of that stuff was, I always just said no, because I was afraid of getting punished.

BE RESPONSIBLE ABOUT YOUR BEHAVIOR

Bow hunting is a very important part of my life. While bow hunting, you must maintain a higher level of awareness of your surroundings and of your behavior. You must understand cause and effect. The discipline I learned from bow hunting helped me to turn down even the most beautiful hippies when they offered me dope. I thought, "Wait a minute—all these people are offering me stuff. But they're puking and stumbling and groveling and they stink and they're acting like complete imbeciles. It's probably the dope! It's probably the alcohol!" I knew this was something to stay away from.

ACTING DECENT IS JUST AS MUCH FUN
AS ACTING HORRIBLE

When I was considered the "Motor City Madman," people wondered how I managed to conduct myself in a responsible manner—and why I bothered. But I knew I needed to pay attention to my band—and I had to pay attention when I was hunting. The high that comes from playing music, combined with the stealthy higher-level awareness that comes from being a predator with a bow and arrow, is a million times better than the cheap thrill you get with alcohol or drugs. I'm telling you, at fifty-six, those observations and conclusions are irrefutable. Just ask Ozzy!

By the time I was in my mid- to late twenties, I was able to tell my dad how much his advice meant to me. Whenever we were in a hunting camp together, I reminded him of how much I loved my lifestyle. Today, if you meet any one of my four children or my grandchildren, you'll see that they're polite, decent, fine, courteous, thoughtful, generous, and attentive human beings, right down to my little one-year-old grandson, Larry. None of my children would ever act out, because they too feared punishment in their childhood, and ultimately they learned that acting decent is just as much fun as acting horrible. My family's sense of personal responsibility has guided us all to an absolutely splendid American dream.

BILL O'REILLY

JOURNALIST AND HOST, *THE O'REILLY FACTOR*

★ ★ ★

When I need advice about the most sensitive decisions in my life, I often turn to Bill O'Reilly. With his big heart, keen insight, and no-bull common sense, he has steered me in the right direction time and time again. At work, he is able to cut through murky issues to shine a light on what is really important. As a former history teacher, he understands what has made our country great in the past, and what threatens that greatness now; he sees it as his job to fight against what could destroy our nation. On a daily basis, I see the love he has for America and his determination to right what is wrong. Bill is a man of principle and a loyal friend. Simply put, he is a rare individual.

PAY ATTENTION TO THOSE YOU ADMIRE

Very few people have given me advice in my life, because I was always a go-my-own-way kind of guy. When you take that approach, you don't tend to get a lot of advice from people. Besides, other people's opinions never would have resonated with me, because I was always an independent thinker.

However, I did watch people closely. I admired people who made it on their own, and I would pay attention to people who started with nothing and built themselves a career. Then I would ask them questions to find out how they got from Point A to Point B. Early on in my career, I made a special quest to talk to Tom Snyder, who was an anchorman for NewsCenter 4, a local New York channel's news program. I thought he was great. I knew he was Irish and came from Milwaukee, went to Marquette University, and was a working guy who made it big. I wanted to find out from Tom exactly how he did it. It took me a while to get in to see him, but I was persistent. I asked him how he went from being a student at Marquette University to being an anchorman in New York. I wanted to know what his progression was. And he was kind enough to walk me through it, step by step.

So my way of going about life has always been a very practical one. I never read the stupid self-help books about the "art of war," by some lame guy who said you had to kill your enemy. I never wanted to do that. Basically, I wanted to find a creative route to success.

DON'T CONFIDE IN A LOT OF PEOPLE

My father's advice was very sparse and to the point—quite pithy, in fact. "Nobody really cares about you but your family," he told me. "Always remember that. If you have two or three good friends in your life you'll be lucky. Don't confide in a lot of people." I didn't take the advice, which was foolish. Sure enough, every time I confided in somebody, particularly about matters in the workplace, I got burned. I didn't wise up until my mid-thirties. If I'd followed my father's advice, and been circumspect with what I told people, I would have been a lot better off.

REPLACE A NEGATIVE THOUGHT WITH A POSITIVE ONE

I also learned an important life lesson from reading. Even though I'm Catholic, I like to read about Eastern philosophy. I'm interested in Eastern thought, because people over there have a totally different mindset than Westerners. I came across a book called *Tantra for the West*. Tantra is a basic way of viewing life; it holds that whenever a negative thought enters your mind, you should accept the thought instead of fighting it. Then you should immediately replace the negative thought with a positive one.

Think about that: Everybody has negative thoughts. Most of us have them all day long. We're afraid, we're insecure, and we worry about what will happen next. Everybody has those thoughts. According to Tantric philosophy, it's natural and normal to have those thoughts. You don't need to take a pill or go to a psychiatrist to talk about these negative thoughts, because they're natural. What you need to do is *accept* them. Don't make your body rigid while trying to fight it, because it's impossible. The positive thought you replace it with can be about anything.

When I decided to try this, I was working in Boston, Massachusetts. Like many news people, just before I'd go on the air I'd wonder, "What if I screw up?" and I'd get tense. It's like a baseball player approaching the plate wondering if he's going to strike out. Using Tantric philosophy, that person should tell himself that he's going to hit a home run—and then relax. So that day, just before I went onto the news set, I got a little apprehensive the way I usually did. But then, as soon as that thought entered my mind, I told myself, "No, I'm going to be extra good tonight. In fact, I'm going to be sensational." That's how I replaced the bad thoughts with the good. And you know what? I was sensational—because I was more relaxed.

After that, every time that I screwed up on the air, I would tell myself that it didn't really matter because people don't pay that close attention— unless you're throwing up or something. If you hesitate a little bit, it won't even be noticed, because everybody hesitates that way. My performance improved 100 percent. Now I'm one of the best in the world on television because I don't care. When I go on every day, I tell myself I'm going to be great—so that negativity doesn't even exist in my mind.

DONNY OSMOND

POP SINGER

I vividly recall the Christmas as a little girl when I got a Donny Osmond album. I was thrilled and surprised—because it was, quite honestly, the coolest gift my parents had ever picked out! I guess my parents thought his squeaky-clean image made it a safe choice.

Despite the years that have passed since, Donny Osmond is still quite like the young boy we all remember. And his music continues to be a safe choice for younger listeners. Rolling Stone *recently wrote a very positive review of Donny's music. And the decades of hit songs continue.*

SURROUND YOURSELF WITH THE BEST

Some of the greatest advice I received in my youth came from my father, George Virl Osmond Sr. He was born on October 13, 1917, and had a very difficult childhood. He was raised by his stepdad and left home at a young age, eventually becoming a sergeant in the army. My father was a dreamer when he was young. He was laughed at; people told him that he'd never amount to anything. Not very many people knew the name Osmond back in 1917. After so many years of work, it's amazing to think of what he's done.

We need more dreamers, but more important, we need more people like my father, who work hard to achieve their dreams. He always dreamed of becoming successful one day, despite the negativity around him. He was a tough father and instilled a hard-working ethic within all nine of his children. I will always admire him because his advice came more through example rather than words.

My father surrounded me with successful people. His philosophy was that a person is more likely to be a success in life when they have a chance to learn from, and associate with, the best. The experience of growing up in show business while surrounded by some of the greatest entertainers in the business was an education in itself. I treasure my diploma from the School of Hard Knocks. I've had my fair share of good and bad times, but I've come to know that practical experience teaches much more than any textbook ever can.

TREASURE YOUR FAILURES, BUT DON'T MAKE THE SAME MISTAKE TWICE

Some may think that this roller-coaster life called show business is filled with nothing but success and glamour. Yes, I have had a very exciting life, and there have been some wonderful moments, but let's not overlook the failures. I treasure those times just as much as the successes, because failure can be the impetus to success—if you allow it. Just make sure you don't make the same mistake twice.

A setback can give you character. It defines who you really are and what you're made of. Sometimes we may be told to make our sights, goals, and dreams more realistic, but I think we should never stop dreaming and aiming high. After all, sometimes our dreams can be accomplished in a slightly different fashion from what we first expect. When I was nine years old, for instance, I had an ambition to be one of the first singers on the moon. Totally unrealistic, some would say. Not long after that, I was told that during one of the Apollo missions they took a recording of Andy Williams with them and left the tape up there. I was singing in the background on that tape. My voice is sitting somewhere on the moon! Not exactly what I had envisioned as a boy, but certainly close to it.

Randy Owen and his dog, Tar Top

RANDY OWEN

LEAD SINGER, ALABAMA

Forty-two number one singles, 65 million records sold, twenty-two multiplat-
inum, platinum, and gold albums, countless awards, and a star on the Holly-
wood Walk of Fame all prove that Alabama is one of the most successful bands in
history. But the group is equally well known for its charitable endeavors.

The band's lead singer, Randy Owen, has always stood out in my eyes as a
rare person. Randy literally started with nothing, and when he gained fame and
fortune he used it to improve other people's lives. When I've been fortunate
enough to spend time with Randy or chatted on the phone with his wife, Kelly,
I've been struck by how sincere and truly caring they are. In fact, Randy has
helped raise more than $60 million for St. Jude Children's Research in Memphis.
If I could sing, I'd sing his praises.

FINISH SCHOOL

I was raised up as poor as you could be, although we had a lot of love and understanding in our home. I had a great mother and a great father, but we just didn't have any money. I mean, *no* money. There were a lot of events that led to who I am, and they all started when I was sixteen years old, when my daddy got really sick. He couldn't help with the harvest, so I dropped out of school and all the farming and harvesting was basically left up to me. I had to pick all the corn and take it to the market; there was just no time for classes. School had always been pretty easy for me; I spent only two weeks in second grade before they sent me to third grade. Now that was all gone.

One day I ran into Mary Ellis, the principal of the elementary school I had attended. I'll never second-guess the reason why, but she took an interest in me and took the time to go back and check my grades in grammar school. Then one day, she asked me, "Randy, why did you drop out of school?" I told her that it was because Daddy had been sick, and besides that, all my friends had dropped out, too. She told me she wanted me back in school. I asked her if she really thought I could get back in and keep up, and she said sure. She was very encouraging.

LEARN TO CONTROL YOUR EMOTIONS

Before I dropped out, I'd been at Fort Payne High School—and, as it turned out, they weren't really open to the idea of letting me start back up in January. I'd missed a lot during the harvest season. But Mrs. Ellis was persistent. I went down to meet with the principal a couple of times. He was discouraging, because I'm sure I didn't look like someone he wanted back in school. I was a really dark-skinned, black-eyed, long-haired guy with dirt on my hands from working on the farm. I was mean; I didn't fear anybody. I was the kind of guy who was always looking for a fight. But I was also embarrassed telling people that I was a high school dropout. Somehow, with God's mercy and wisdom, Mary Ellis and I persuaded them to let me back in—and on my first test I scored 99½. The teacher was shocked. I graduated from high school in about three years.

I remember what it feels like to be different from most of the other kids, because I looked different. From my work on the farm, my hands always looked dirty. I just couldn't get them clean. My shoes and clothes were torn and we couldn't afford new ones. But, you know, through the gift of hardship I learned how to control my emotions, and how to ignore taunts and jabs. In the end, that's probably the best thing I learned at school.

DON'T BE DETERRED BY DISCOURAGEMENT

Getting through high school gave me a lot of encouragement. "Well, if I can go through this," I thought, "I can surely get my college degree." I went through two years of junior college, then transferred to Jacksonville State University and got my degree. All I really ever wanted to do was play the guitar and sing. But, thanks to the help I'd gotten from Mary Ellis, I also got my education. Many times in my life people have looked down on me, but I always knew I was smart. I just needed a chance to prove it.

I always loved music. My daddy taught me to play guitar, my mother played piano, and we'd sing in church together. So when I got older I figured, if I can do that, then I can go out and stand on a stage and play my guitar. The music business was tough. In the beginning, everyone was discouraging me. But by then I was so used to being turned away or underestimated in my early childhood that it didn't deter me.

DON'T FEEL YOU HAVE TO BE LIKE EVERYONE ELSE

By 1980, I knew things were starting to happen for our group, Alabama. My wife, Kelly, and I had flown back home, and my parents picked us up. We were sitting in the car and I said, "Daddy, it looks like my dreams are about to start coming true." And he said, "Well, you put a lot into it. It's about time." Shortly thereafter he passed away. It was true: I got my education, even though most everyone else I knew didn't. I stuck with it. When I went into the music business, I did the same. Today, I tell kids, "Get your degree, but then don't feel you have to be like everyone else. When I was in school, I was always different. It may not feel like it, but that can be a blessing." Now I encourage kids to be different, if that's what they feel. They don't have to become a doctor or lawyer or businessman. There have to be people like me to make the world go 'round.

Dr. Mehmet Oz (right) *with his father and daughter*

DR. MEHMET OZ

SURGEON AND AUTHOR OF *YOU:*
THE OWNER'S MANUAL

★ ★ ★

My first glimpse of Dr. Mehmet Oz was through the back window of a tour bus in France, when he was acting very un-doctor-like. While I won't go into detail, what he was doing had everyone in stitches—that is, in laughter.

Mehmet is unlike any doctor I'd ever met; within days of meeting him I knew I'd made a lifelong friend. He is a professor and vice chairman of surgery at Columbia University, and medical director of the Integrated Medicine Center and director of the Heart Institute at New York Presbyterian/Columbia Medical Center. He has written over 350 articles and books, including his latest number one New York Times *bestseller,* You: The Owner's Manual. *Although his degrees are from Harvard, the University of Pennsylvania School of Medicine, and Wharton Business School, Mehmet incorporates alternative ideas about physical and mental health into traditional Western techniques. He treats patients with Eastern therapies as well as the latest Western procedures.*

But what I love best is that he uses laughter as an important ingredient in his healthy living regimen.

ENCOURAGE, INSPIRE, AND LEAD

I went to a private school in Delaware. We played sports there, but we were never very good. I didn't understand the mind of an athlete. During those years playing football in high school and then in college, I came to realize that you have to become comfortable with yourself to be able to play sports at any level—and you have to understand what it means to be a leader. I can still remember running off the field in high school and telling my football coach I was exhausted. The heat was stifling. He looked at me and said, "I never want to hear you say that in front of the other players." What he was saying was, "I understand you're tired, and I do feel for you, but that's not the message we're going to send out right now. The message we're going to send out is that we are all hustling, and we are all doing our best. So you're going to say you're feeling all right because that's what the team needs to hear." I had to get used to being uncomfortable. I had a job to do, which was to encourage and inspire and lead my team. It became very clear that there are certain things that you need to keep to yourself if you're going to play a leadership position.

BE COMFORTABLE WITH BEING UNCOMFORTABLE

While I'm not an athlete now, I believe that the same advice pertains to surgeons. As a surgeon, folks look to you for leadership. So you need to be an unfailing optimist and you need to demonstrate responsibility and selfless dedication. My patients don't care if I'm tired or if I've had a bad day. Part of being a professional is always putting their needs before mine. That can produce side effects that aren't always positive, in terms of keeping the healer well, but it is an important credo. That football coach taught me to be a leader. The phrase I think is important is, "You have to be comfortable with being uncomfortable." It's okay not to be happy, not to have everything go your way, not to be in perfect control of everything. In surgery, as in sports, in every procedure there is a time when you don't have control. You have to find the flow and get into it so that you can do your best in any situation. You have to be a leader.

DON'T MICROMANAGE

It's the same in many professions. In a high-quality kitchen, the chef doesn't cook every dish. The chef can't micromanage everybody who is working under him. For a leader, the biggest hurdle is learning how to let go and realize that you can't do everything yourself. It's also about learning the simple life lesson that you're going to compete against someone who is better than you one day and worse than you the next. Other things are going to happen that you dislike. In life there are going to be times when you don't control all the variables, but you have to be comfortable with not being where you want to be all the time and still be able to function. This approach should continue throughout your life and career.

CRAFT AN ORCHESTRA

The Achilles' heel of many great leaders is that they don't take the time to teach the next generation how to prosper. In the surgical profession, the saying is "You eat your young." You don't let them prosper because your ego gets in the way. Great leaders desire to be perfectionists, but they have to recognize that perfection lies not in themselves and doing everything perfectly. Rather, great leaders create harmony by crafting an orchestra, rather than a cacophony of musicians.

LEARN TO CREATE A CONTINGENCY PLAN

You also need irrational optimism to be a great leader. This should come about not because you believe your own press, but because you recognize that truly important things are going to come out of it. You can't get caught up in believing that if you miss a point the world will collapse, or if you miss a surgical stitch it's the end of mankind. The calmest I have ever felt, in the operating room and on the sports field, is when I realized that I had people around me whom I could trust. I always had another opportunity. I always gave myself more chances. By relying on the help of others, I know that I can create a contingency plan.

A SENSE OF BALANCE

I use yoga to deal with stress in my life. In yoga, the most important thing is to work on the central element of breathing. That's your core essence. You always breathe no matter what your body's doing. It doesn't matter how extreme your position is, you must always be balanced. Great leaders often have that sense of balance.

I'll never forget what happened to one young surgeon I knew. He was a pretty talented man, but in the middle of an operation his patient started hemorrhaging blood and all hell broke out. He panicked and yelled, "Someone help me. Anybody. Get someone to help me." I've felt like that many times, but you have to reach back to the deeper sense of who you are and calm yourself. When that surgeon said those words, he destroyed his ability to lead those people—because he lost confidence in himself.

DOLLY PARTON

COUNTRY MUSIC SINGER AND ACTRESS

★ ★ ★

One thing I've learned in working on this book is that rich kids don't have a lock on future success. Dolly Parton was the fourth of twelve children growing up in a one-room cabin in Tennessee. Early in her career, she was pigeonholed as a country-and-western singer. Before long, though, Dolly Parton proved that no one could typecast her. Starring in 9 to 5, *Parton stole the show from her fellow actresses and the title song became a major hit for her, earning her Golden Globe and Academy Award nominations, two Grammys, and the number one spot on the Billboard Hot 100. Major roles in* The Best Little Whorehouse in Texas, Straight Talk, *and* Steel Magnolias *soon followed.*

Dolly Parton is equally famous for being a shrewd businesswoman in a very tough business. That in itself makes her amazing. And she has given back to the traditionally poor part of Appalachia through Dollywood, the theme park that draws visitors from across America.

FILL UP YOUR IMAGE BANK

My daddy didn't have much education, but his great horse-sense advice was invaluable. He once told me, "The more successful you are, the more value your name, likeness, and endorsement have to others. It's as if, with each special thing you do, you're filling up your image bank. Any time you decide to endorse someone else's product or service, that too should put value in your image bank. If it doesn't, it was a bad decision. If it does, then the next product or service you endorse will be worth even more."

Many artists and entertainers have depleted their image bank and their actual bank accounts by taking up a "cause" or trying to sell products just because they earned a royalty or a commission. Anyway, that's why you seldom see me selling anything except myself and my own things . . . like Dollywood, Dixie Stampede, and, of course, my music.

JEANINE PIRRO

DISTRICT ATTORNEY OF WESTCHESTER COUNTY,
NEW YORK

★ ★ ★

As I write this, Jeanine Pirro is the district attorney of Westchester County, which is just north of New York City. But she has also just announced that she will run for the U.S. Senate seat currently held by Hillary Clinton. Within New York State, she's popular. She's also tenacious. Her office prosecutes more than thirty thousand people a year. Jeanine reminds me of Emma Peel in The Avengers: *She's a glamorous woman who often sports stiletto heels and has even appeared on* People's *50 Most Beautiful People list, but she is also a determined avenger of victims. As a district attorney, she's a sex offender's or wife-beater's worst nightmare. She impressed me before she became a friend because she is a woman gutsier than most men I know and ferocious in her attempts to right wrongs, to help victims, and to lock up bad guys.*

HELP PEOPLE WHO CAN'T HELP THEMSELVES

My mom was in the grocery store in our little town of Elmira, New York, when she met a woman who was blind. The woman was trying to gather her bags, and it was clear to my mother that she needed some help. She struck up a conversation, and the next Friday there we were, my mother and I, going to pick up Mrs. Labert to go grocery shopping. I remember pulling up to her house. My first reaction was shock. She lived in an old home, not an apartment. I can still see the dingy shades; as we entered, I was struck by how dark it was. There were big stacks of things scattered throughout the house. It wasn't that the house was dirty, it was just messy—until you got to the kitchen. In the kitchen, there was order. Everything was in its place because of the danger if something were to come too close to the stove while she was cooking.

Soon, our trips to help Mrs. Labert became a weekly routine. We'd pick her up, go shopping, help put away the groceries, and then get her ready for the new week. She was a lovely, articulate woman with snow-white hair that she wore up in pins. Growing up, I thought everyone was as generous and thoughtful as my mother. I was a little girl, certainly younger than ten, and my mother's concern for this woman who was not a relative, not even a long-time friend, left an indelible impression on me.

When I asked my mother why she did this, she said, "You have to help people who can't help themselves." This vivid picture of my mother helping Mrs. Labert has made an impact on my life and my fight to level the playing field for battered women, seniors, and abused children. I translated my mother's social philosophy into a criminal justice philosophy.

HELP WHERE YOU ARE NEEDED

I also recall Mrs. Fleming—or, more specifically, Mrs. Fleming's hair. She was a wonderful elderly lady who lived near our house. She had a big Victorian porch, but she couldn't walk very well, and certainly couldn't lift her arms over her head. So every Saturday morning my mother sent me to wash Mrs. Fleming's hair. We didn't have hot rollers then, so I had put in those little pin curls, and because we didn't have blow-dryers I had to wait until Saturday night, go back over, and take the pins out of Mrs. Fleming's hair. Even though I loved to help Mrs. Fleming, I did discover at an early age that I didn't want to be a hairdresser!

HELP THE VICTIM

From the time I first saw Perry Mason on TV when I was very young, I knew I was going to be an attorney. But for me the underdog wasn't the person who was wrongly accused, it was the person who was abused or neglected. It was clear to me when I became a prosecutor that my mission was to help the victim, the person who never chose to be a victim in the first place. The hallmark of my career has really been my philosophy that our obligation in criminal justice is not just to make criminals accountable, but to try to make victims whole again—whether that victim is an abused child who wasn't believed, a senior citizen who is being conned because he or she is old and vulnerable, or someone who's a victim of a hate crime.

GET INVOLVED

In some ways, I see myself carrying out the same job that my mother started when she helped Mrs. Labert, who had found herself in a situation where she couldn't do it alone. Recently, my mom gave me a note that Mrs. Labert had written her before she died. She had only become blind later in life, so she could still write, and though her penmanship was crooked, her spirit shined through. There were tears in my mother's eyes when she gave it to me. It read:

> *To Esther*
> *Though my eyes cannot see your face*
> *My heart has clearly seen*
> *That goodness dwells in you with grace.*
> *You've made me feel a queen.*
> *Bon Voyage now, little friend,*
> *My prayer will follow you*
> *Until you reach your journey's end*
> *. . . and then begin anew.*

Most people would simply have walked away from Mrs. Labert in that store and said, "She's blind. That's the way it is." But not my mother. She never settled for the way things were. Whenever she thought she could help people, she always got involved.

GIVE OF YOURSELF AND YOUR TIME

I remember once being in an ice cream shop in Elmira and a senior citizen came in and the first thing my sister and I did was get up so that that person could sit down. That's just the way we were raised. It's not something you think about. It's not about manners, it's about trying to make things better for people who aren't in as good a position as you are.

I think that kind of respect and human decency is lacking today. Our culture is developing a philosophy of not getting involved, and it's eroding our society. We are starting to look the other way when we could lend a hand. If you give us a 9/11 or a tsunami, we all reach into our pockets and make ourselves feel better. But how many of us do what my mother did every week for Mrs. Labert? How many of us give people our time, or sit in a dark room and talk to a woman who is lonely and has no family left? We don't give of ourselves, we merely give things. My mother taught me to give of myself, and I think that's what I do in my job. As tough as we are and as hard as we work to put criminals in jail, we work even harder to try and make their victims whole again, to try and piece them back together, to try to turn back the hands of time as best we can.

OPEN YOUR HEART AND SOUL

I understand that many people don't have a lot of time to share, but it's also about sharing your heart. If we open our hearts and our souls, it's so much more powerful than opening our wallets. That's what my mother taught me. Today we forget how a kind word can make another person's day. We forget how a certain amount of gentleness in people's lives—especially those who have been battered, abused, conned, or ignored—can change them and add some brightness to their days.

BILL RICHARDSON

GOVERNOR OF NEW MEXICO

Bill Richardson has been called a traveling troubleshooter. Indeed, whether serving in a national, state, or local position, he's made foreign policy and security issues a top priority. As a governor, he met with a North Korean delegation to discuss concerns over that country's nuclear ambitions. He's visited Cuba, Peru, Nigeria, Nicaragua, Bangladesh, and more. He has served as a congressman, U.S. secretary of energy, U.S. ambassador to the United Nations, and now as the governor of New Mexico. He is a Democrat who proposed tax cuts to promote growth and investment. He was able to pass a personal income tax cut, started special tax-free shopping days for purchases under $2,500 to stimulate small business sales, and made New Mexico the first state in the nation to provide $250,000 in life insurance for national guardsmen on active duty. Governor Richardson is so widely admired that he was named chairman of the 2004 Democratic National Convention and chairman of the Democratic Governors Association.

HAVE AN EXTRA EDGE

My father drilled into me the importance of outworking anybody else. He stressed the importance of respecting other cultures, and learning English and Spanish at the same time. He wasn't somebody who offered much in the way of overt affection, and when I was trying to get better grades or become a better athlete, I always found myself struggling to please him. In a way, though, he was giving me an incentive to become an even better and more successful person. He was in his sixties when I was born, so we had two generational gaps dividing us. At the time we were living in Mexico; if I were going to compete in the United States in academics and athletics, he felt, I would have to have an extra edge, to strive more intensively to reach my goals. He knew I'd have to be extra good if I were going to go to the big leagues of sports, politics, or academics.

WORK HARD, BROADEN YOURSELF, AND HAVE A THICK SKIN

One time, I showed my father a report in the newspaper that mentioned me—because I had moved from tenth best in my baseball league to second best, and the only player ahead of me was older. "Look!" I said. "I've gone from tenth to second!" He replied, "Well, I want you to be first." Then, in the last game of the season, I overtook the guy to win the batting title. My father still didn't say much. I knew he was proud of me, but he would never tell me. It wasn't always easy to have a father who was so hard to please. But that instilled in me a very hard work ethic and strong competitive streak and an interest in broadening myself.

Because of my upbringing, I developed a thick skin very early on. It has certainly been helpful in politics, where the slings and arrows come fast and from every direction. It's something that has made me a better political leader, but a political leader also needs to develop a better connection with his people. I feel that connection with those I work with, but sometimes I don't show it enough. I've been in public life for thirty years, and on the average somebody attacks me in the newspaper once a day. Even on non-news days there's always something negative about me in the press. That's why a thick skin has served me well.

PLAN FOR YOUR FUTURE

When I was in college at Tufts in Massachusetts, I was drifting aimlessly. I was a good athlete, but I didn't know what I wanted to do as a profession, and I was a mediocre student. My interests were baseball, dating, and my fraternity. I had no idea what I wanted to do when I grew up.

But there was one individual—a young dean at the Fletcher School named Arthur House—who gave a speech to my fraternity. I was the president of the frat, and we'd often have people come in to give speeches telling us how we should be better people. He said to me, "You know two lan-guages. You understand two cultures. You need to make your fraternity more relevant by doing charity work instead of just drinking beer." I was a pretty decent baseball player, but my arm was basically dead, and I realized I'd have to start planning for a different future. So I was under some pressure to do something with my life. In that one encounter, Arthur House had a pro-found impact on me; he made me think about international affairs, and about life. I later returned the favor by supporting him in a run for Congress.

DEDICATE YOURSELF TO PUBLIC SERVICE

Around the same time, I went with one of my classes to the Senate chambers to hear Hubert Humphrey give a speech. He said, "There's nothing more gratifying than a life of public service and helping people through that ser-vice." The speech was about poverty in Africa and poverty in America, and how we could all do something about both if we dedicated ourselves to pub-lic service. That message helped me solidify my decision to run for office and go into government.

STICK WITH IT

I can't discount my wife's impact on my life. She is always proven right. When she tells me it's not the time to run for an office, I listen to her. I wanted to run for governor before, and she told me to stay in Congress. I had a huge disappointment in 1992; I was supposed to be named secretary of the interior by President Clinton, but the environmentalists killed my nomina-tion because I wasn't green enough for them. I remember being very disap-pointed and thinking of retiring from Congress. But my wife told me, "Better things will come, so stick with it." It was during that time that I worked on all those rescues of the American servicemen and the hostages. It's her judgment that keeps me grounded and focused on what to seek and what to try to achieve. This morning, she asked me to talk to the legislature about funds for domestic violence, and I did. She is the one with the harder edge. She is not only my wife; she is my closest political adviser.

Cathy Rigby with daughters Jude (left) *and Hailey*

CATHY RIGBY

SPORTSCASTER AND ACTRESS

★ ★ ★

Think of what you were doing at age sixteen, and then compare it to what Cathy Rigby was doing. At that young age, Cathy had already made the U.S. Olympic team for the 1968 Olympics in Mexico City; while she was there she became the highest-scoring U.S. gymnast. The public's love affair with Cathy began that year, and it has continued ever since. Her star quality was confirmed when she won gold that same year at the World Cup. By the time she was eighteen, she was the gold medalist at the U.S. Championships. At the World Cup in 1971 she took the gold again, and was the World Cup all-around champion. The following year she was back on the U.S. Olympic team. When she retired from competitive sports in 1972, Cathy began an eighteen-year career as a commentator for ABC Sports. She also performed in stage performances of Annie Get Your Gun, Meet Me in St. Louis, *and* The Wizard of Oz, *and was nominated for a Tony for her role as Peter Pan on Broadway. Equally important, in the early 1980s, when the disorder was largely unknown, Cathy Rigby went public with her battle against bulimia, and spoke publicly about her experiences with this life-threatening disease.*

JUST DO IT

My life was formed by people who wouldn't take no for an answer when faced with challenges. The best example is my mother, who is a unique individual. She lost her mother—my grandmother—to tuberculosis when she was just nine years old. Her father lost everything in the stock market crash. Her brother died in World War II. Then when she was pregnant with my older brother, she was diagnosed with polio. Through it all, she worked and raised five kids! She is an amazing woman in that she was very affected by her polio and yet I never ever saw my mother as handicapped in any way. I just assumed she could do anything she wanted to do and be anything she wanted to be. Even to this day, at the age of seventy-seven, she is one of those people who just does it all. She is the living example of the Nike motto: "Just Do It."

NEVER GIVE UP

By pure luck, at the age of ten, I found gymnastics. It wasn't something I wanted to do for the rest of my life. I certainly never thought I was going to be an Olympic gymnast. I just loved the sport and was fortunate enough to have a mother who said "Go do it," and a great coach who helped me get it done. I think my mother's example of never giving up really changed my life. "Even if you don't have what in the beginning appears to be all the talent in the world," she said, "you can surpass any limitation." If someone had told me I would accomplish anything in the Olympics—or in the theater—I would have thought they were out of their minds, that there was no way on God's green earth that I would reach the level I did. But somewhere along the way, I just did it. That little echo in my ear of my mother saying *you can do it* made all the difference in the world.

PERSISTENCE, HARD WORK, AND BELIEVING IN YOURSELF

I vividly recall one young girl on my gymnastics team. She was very overweight and the only thing she really had going for her was flexibility. But I watched as this girl, through sheer willpower, made it to the national level. I was so impressed by her. I truly believe that—more than talent—persistence, hard work, and sheer willpower will make you get better. You have to have a compulsive desire to be great. Yet it's hard to have that kind of intense attitude. I laugh, because it's the thing that can also get you in trouble, because those of us who have it are usually obsessive-compulsive in other areas. The struggle is taking that God-given drive and putting it to good work.

KEEP FOCUSED ON WHO YOU ARE

It was also incredibly important that my mother was always proud of me, whether I was winning or losing. Because gymnastics is such a pressure-filled sport, I think my mother's unconditional acceptance was my saving grace and perhaps what kept me sane. I never had to ask my parents if they were proud of me. I always knew they were. There was so much pressure everywhere else that being able to come home and relax was great. Athletes spend all that time training because they love what they do and want to be good at it. But too often, gymnastics becomes about what you do, not about who you are. In the Olympics, you have one chance every four years to prove yourself. You never know what you're going to feel like on that day; the pressure is mind-numbing. Afterward, though, you can look back and know that if you can do that, you can do anything.

YOU DON'T DO ANYTHING ALONE

In a way, my mother's handicap strengthened me. When you see your mother struggling with a wheelchair and crutches, unable to stand up or go to the bathroom, it puts everything in perspective very quickly. That's very healthy. Before competitions, my mom didn't go into long motivational speeches; she was just a great example. Before each competition she was probably as nervous as every other parent, but she wasn't living through my accomplishments. She was happy for me. When I won at the world championships in Yugoslavia, I remember being on the victory stand with a medal around my neck and my mom and my dad and coach all behind me as the flag went up. You don't do anything alone; we accomplished this together. It was great to share that moment with them.

REMEMBER THE SACRIFICE OF OTHERS

I can't leave out my four siblings. They all sacrificed for me, because we knew that if we were going to spend more money on what I needed, there would be less to go around. I took them for granted back then, because as a kid you're so involved in your own things, but I look back now and realize that I have the most amazing brothers and sisters.

Then again, maybe they were glad it was me and not them, considering the immense amount of time and hard work that goes into training!

From left: *Geraldo Rivera with Kurt Vonnegut, Dr. Henry Kissinger, and Frank Sinatra*

GERALDO RIVERA

TELEVISION JOURNALIST

There is no one like Geraldo. He is impossible to miss in a crowd . . . no matter how large the crowd! When I worked at Eyewitness News *in New York, though it was many years after Geraldo, the stories about him—on and off camera— were legendary. His work exposing horrific abuse of mentally retarded patients at Willowbrook School in New York was one of the finest pieces of investigative journalism in broadcast history.*

Despite his incredible reporting, though, the public image of Geraldo over- shadowed his award winning work. His daytime self-named talk show was a must-watch, just to see what crazy stunt he was going to pull next. Who can for- get the show Geraldo did about the opening of Al Capone's secret vault? The only secret was that it was empty, yet the show garnered the highest ratings for a syndi- cated special in TV history.

Now that I've worked with Geraldo for five years and spent wonderful time with him and his wife, Erica, I've seen a completely different side of him. Ger- aldo lives, works, and plays at the speed of light; yet, when a friend is in need, he's there. Many people don't know that his brother, Craig, is his cameraman. So when you see Geraldo getting shot at in Tora Bora, Afghanistan, the person who keeps recording as bullets whiz overhead is Craig. Craig would never run; Ger- aldo can always trust him to stick by his side even if the going gets tough. Geraldo is the same way. He is loyal, dedicated, and kind to a fault.

GET A TICKET OUT

My father's struggle in life was my main motivation to succeed. He got up at 4:30 every morning and never had any energy or any time, because he worked double shifts at a defense plant. We never had enough money. My mom was a cashier at Corvettes, which was kind of an early Wal-Mart. They always wanted me to get an education.

But there were four main people whose advice ultimately changed my life. The first was my high school principal, Russell Van Brunt, from West Babylon High School. He'd been a navy captain in World War II, stationed in Guam and Puerto Rico. Since we were the only Puerto Rican family in West Babylon, he took on a special affection for us.

In those years, I was going the wrong way. My grades were okay, and I was an athlete, but I was also in two gangs. The first was the Valve Grinders, a car-oriented gang; the other, the Corner Boys, was really a turf-brawling kind of gang. Mr. Van Brunt saw what was happening to me: I was heading to a dead end. So he gave me two bits of advice. "Number one," he said, "get off Long Island. Number two, go to Fort Schuyler, the State University of New York Maritime College, and get in the Navy Reserve. That's a good ticket out." That really made all the difference. I went to SUNY Maritime College, and it broadened my horizons; it made me a sailor, and made me familiar with the military. It gave me a whole different mindset. Just getting out of that hood made all the difference. Plus, it helped just knowing that he cared about me.

TAKE A LONG-TERM VIEW OF LIFE

The second important person was my father-in-law, Harry Coblentz. I married his daughter, Linda, as soon as I graduated from the University of Arizona in 1965. That summer he said, "Why don't we have a little heart-to-heart?" I'd spent some time selling clothing between Maritime College and the University of Arizona, and knew I could make a living at it. I was a good salesman. Instead, he said, "Why don't you think about going to law school? You speak well. You've always been coherent in your arguments. You're not afraid to speak out. That's a perfect way to channel that energy." I hadn't thought about that at all. I went out to L.A. for the summer, and then in '66 decided to drive back to New York, where I took the LSAT and applied for law school. In that one moment, my father-in-law had given me a long-term view of my life—and changed it forever.

TO DESTROY IS EASY, TO REFORM IS TOUGH

When I went to law school, I became a very radicalized thinker. I represented a group called the Young Lords and a lot of other radical groups, many of which were involved in actions against city institutions. One of the institutions we frequently protested was the City University of New York, which was run by Vice Chancellor Julius C. C. Edelstein, who had been a deputy mayor under Robert Wagner and a naval officer. At one point, he pulled me aside and said, "To destroy is easy. To tear down is easy. Tyrants can do that. If you're interested in social change, why don't you figure out a way to go from being a revolutionary to being a reformer, from being a destroyer to being a crafter?" He was right. If you want to institute reform in the rules of tenure, I realized, or you want to get more minorities recruited as professors, why not work on that, rather than tearing down an institution that does some good, however flawed? He was the third person who gave me advice that turned me around. His words helped guide me from being a wild '60s activist to a much more sober, constructive, progressive person.

YOU'RE NOT GOING TO BE
A ROCK STAR FOREVER

Then, in 1994, when I was in the middle of my very successful daytime show, Roger Ailes came to me and asked, "How long will you want to do this? How long do you want to do a show about *My daughter's a hooker,* then the next day, *My granddaughter's a hooker too,* followed up by, *My grandmother was also a hooker?* There's much more in you. You're much brighter than that." And he made me an offer: "I'm starting this thing called CNBC, and I want you there." So I tried out, but he caught on that I was having trouble seeing the teleprompter. So he said, "Don't be afraid to wear your glasses. You're not going to be a rock star forever. If you can't read without your glasses, put your glasses on."

ASK YOURSELF, WHAT'S IN IT FOR THEM?

I honor all four of those guys. The choices I made, based on the advice from all of them, helped me to become as successful as I am. By caring about me and looking at me without attitude, but rather with open-mindedness and love and probably at least some curiosity, they guided me. You know, listening to good advice is just as important as getting good advice. You always hear people telling you, *Do this* or *Do that.* When you're young, it usually goes in one ear and out the other. So you have to stop and ask yourself, *What's in it for this person?* If they don't have a particular axe to grind, listen to them, because they probably care about you and want you to do better. I've learned that every once in a while someone hits the right note. The people you pick as your advisers—the ones you decide to trust—make all the difference.

DORIS ROBERTS

ACTRESS

Everybody loves Doris Roberts! She's a multiple award-winning actress with three Emmys (and nominations for many more), an American Comedy Award, and a TV Guide Award. I loved her as secretary Mildred Krebs on the hit NBC series Remington Steele. *Everyone loves her on the smash hit* Everybody Loves Raymond, *where she plays Marie Barone, Ray Romano's nosy mom. And whatever she goes on to do next, we'll love here there, too—in first-run shows and forever in syndication!*

ADJUST THE WAY YOU VIEW PEOPLE

The best advice I got didn't come from a person, but rather from witnessing an age-old tradition. Several years ago, I went to visit the Schramsberg Caves, near Calistoga up in the Napa Valley of California. Schramsberg produces a champagne style of wine in the *méthode champenoise* style—meaning that it's fermented in the bottle. I watched as the workers riddled the wine. That's a process where a worker turns the bottle an eighth or quarter turn per day—a small movement that moves the sediment into the bottle's neck, where it's removed. As the fermentation continues, the garbage in the bottle comes up and they remove it using the pressure of the built-up gas. The result is this wonderful champagne.

When I heard that process described, I wondered how I could do the same with my life. And I found a way to do it—by simply adjusting my sights, ever so slightly, day after day. By adjusting the way you look at those around you, you find that you're able to see them in a different light. You decide what it is about a certain person that you like, and you stick with that image. The rest of it, the negative image, you throw away.

KENNY ROGERS

COUNTRY MUSIC SINGER AND ACTOR

★ ★ ★

Like many country singers, Kenny Rogers comes from humble beginnings. But now Kenny is a hit-making machine, who has been on the pop and country charts since the 1960s. Perhaps more important, Kenny changed the entertainment game when he successfully led the way for other artists to break out of music and into acting, by turning his hit song "The Gambler" into a made-for-TV movie. It became such a smash success that there were multiple sequels. And he didn't stop there: Kenny even started his own fast-food restaurant chain, Kenny Rogers Roasters, which has grown into an international business!

As with so many other celebrities who came from difficult backgrounds, Kenny has devoted himself to philanthropic endeavors of all kinds.

STRIVE FOR MORE BUT BE HAPPY WHERE YOU ARE

My mother, who had dropped out of school after third grade, always told me, "Be happy where you are. Strive for more, but if you don't get there, be happy where you are." I had seven siblings, and our life was pretty humble growing up in Houston. I was never motivated to earn a lot of money, but I really did want to play music. I went to a Ray Charles concert when I was thirteen, and I was amazed to see how people applauded at his music and laughed at his jokes. People will clap for music to be nice, but they won't laugh to be nice. That's how you could tell he really connected. That's when I realized: To truly entertain people, you need to do more than just sing. I guess that always stuck in the back of my mind.

THERE ARE TWO WORDS IN "SHOW BUSINESS"

My older brother was the guy who actually got me into the professional music business. He was a promotion man for a record company, and he got them to cut a record for me when I was nineteen years old. The B-side of that first single, "That Crazy Feeling," got on the radio, and it was popular enough that I got a slot on *American Bandstand*.

I went off to college at the University of Texas, but I dropped out to play bass in the Bobby Doyle Three jazz band. When they broke up, I joined up with a guy named Kirby Stone, a popular light jazz artist. He was a great business philosopher. "There are two words in show business," he told me. "One is show. The other is business. If you don't really treat them both with respect, your career won't last long." If the show starts at eight, he told me, you should start playing at eight, because people respect that.

Kirby took me under his wing; later he took me to L.A. and introduced me to the New Christy Minstrels, a big folk group. During my year and a half with them, I learned so much about putting a show together—about when to step back, what to do when you're on stage, and how to make it all come together. Unfortunately, they wouldn't let me sing on their records, because they already had a formula that worked for them, and I didn't fit in it. It cut the wind out of my sails.

PEOPLE TIE EVENTS TOGETHER

Four of us walked away from the group and formed the First Edition. It was very, very successful for a lot of different reasons. First off, the timing was crucial. Second, the mother of our guitar player, Terry Williams, was the secretary to Jimmy Bowen, who ran Reprise Records. She told her boss, "My son has this little band and I'd love for you to hear them." He signed us— and the First Edition had nine top ten records.

It's funny how people tie events together. Without Kirby Stone, I would never have been with the New Christy Minstrels. Because I met Terry, we created the First Edition. Because of his mom, we got a record deal. I remember our group was playing on *The Ed Sullivan Show* one night, and as we were singing it just struck me that only big stars got to do Ed Sullivan. I thought, "This is pretty cool."

I had a pop-psychedelic song called "Just Dropped In (to See What Condition My Condition Was In)." It was a bizarre song I wrote in the '60s, about an LSD trip. By then, I realized that I wanted to go solo, and the last night the First Edition was together, we played with Dinah Shore. As we were closing, I played "Just Dropped In" for her, and she said, "Now, boy, there's a hit." I thought, "If she thinks it's a hit, I'm running with it." Sure enough, it was a great success.

DON'T LET ONE THING CONSUME YOUR LIFE

I had met Larry Butler in Nashville, and I decided I wanted to do a country album because I'd been raised with country music. In country music, I felt I'd found my home. But I also believe that it's emotionally dangerous to have one thing consume your entire life. I've always felt you need other things you can be equally as passionate about. So I started making movies, acting in TV shows, and all the while enjoying making my music. I try to remember my mother's philosophy about being happy where you are. Try to do better things, but be happy.

The one thing I can honestly tell you is that all my life I've been a happy person. I think that's worth more than any amount of money I could ever make.

MICKEY AND JAN ROONEY

ACTOR AND SINGER

HUSBAND AND WIFE

★ ★ ★

Think of the biggest movie stars of the past twenty years: Julia Roberts, Mel Gibson, Harrison Ford, Tom Cruise, Meryl Streep may come to mind. But their success can't hold a candle to Mickey Rooney's. He has made more than two hundred films—over eight decades! It is almost impossible to believe that any one person could have achieved as much success as he did. When, after a few lower-grossing films, people began to write him off as a has-been, Mickey came back stronger than ever. Between 1939 and 1979 he was nominated for four Academy Awards and was honored with a Lifetime Achievement Oscar. He had five Emmy nominations, won one, and also won two Golden Globe Awards.

Of course, Mickey didn't exactly have the same luck with wives—after all, he's had eight! I can't vouch for the others, but I know that his current wife, Jan, keeps him on the right track. And Mickey knows it, too.

LISTEN TO YOUR WIFE

Mickey: I don't know if I could have appreciated my wife, Jan, early on in my life. It's very difficult when you achieve success in Hollywood, or anywhere else, to find people who really like you for what you are, not for the success you have. I was too mixed up back then. Even when I first met her in 1974, at a party at our agent's house, I didn't realize how special she was. I started talking to her and found out she was a singer, and I asked her for a date. We started going together and soon became engaged.

I changed my life because Jan kept me on the straight and narrow road. I used to be evasive with my career. I didn't know what I really wanted to do. I picked projects that I shouldn't have worked on. But Janice told me, "Put your mind to the situation, and then listen to me." She was right. She made me more decisive. She guides me. She's naturally the type of person who takes charge of the situation. Her best advice was, "Listen to your wife." She's my guiding light. We've been married for thirty years. We have our star together on Hollywood Boulevard for live entertainment. It's a team effort; we consider ourselves the California team.

INCLUDE YOUR SPOUSE
IN EVERYTHING YOU DO

Mickey: I've got news for you, when you're married you should always include your spouse in everything you do. We write songs together, we paint together, and we sing together; it's a team effort. My career was dying when I met Jan, and she brought me back. She was the only one who was really genuinely interested in me. She showed me over and over how much she genuinely cared for me by guiding me and helping me. I can't pick just one great thing that she's done for me, because she's done *everything* for me.

You know, it doesn't matter where we go, so long as we're together. That's the way life is supposed to be. Everyone needs that in life. I'm lucky that I have someone to share my life with now. It's special and it's lovely and it's wonderful. I wouldn't be where I am now without her. We've stuck together through thick and thin. She is the one who tells me when I'm wrong, and I'm wrong about a lot of things. I try to do things that I shouldn't, and she stops me. She's thoughtful, kind, courteous, and she is a perfect lady. She's my inspiration.

DON'T BE AFRAID TO CHANGE
THE CHOICES YOU MAKE

Jan: Mickey felt Hollywood had turned its back on him. He was the number one box office star in the late 1930s and early 1940s. After *National Velvet* in 1944, Mickey enlisted in the army. When he came back, things had changed. Over the years he started feeling like he wasn't wanted any more, and it seemed as if he'd just given up. When we met, I realized that Mickey had made bad choices about the projects he was doing. I wanted him to do *Sugar Babies,* the Broadway play, but he didn't want to. Just as he was signing a contract that would tie him up for two years and prevent him from going to

Broadway and doing the show, I grabbed the pen from the agent and said, "He can't sign this." Of course, *Sugar Babies* was a phenomenal success.

Honestly, sometimes I don't know how we stay together. We fight like little cats and dogs. He had a problem with our horses, and I had to step in and tell him, "That's it. You can't do that anymore." There are periods of light, and then some dark along the way. Sometimes, I just want to strangle him. But we respect each other and love each other, and because of that we stay together through all the tough times.

Secretary of Defense Donald Rumsfeld with E. D. Hill, 2004

DONALD RUMSFELD

UNITED STATES SECRETARY OF DEFENSE

★ ★ ★

I was six months pregnant with my fifth child when I first met Secretary of Defense Donald Rumsfeld. Maybe it was my hormones talking, but I'll confess that I was shocked at my reaction. Yes, he's interesting, witty, wry, and confident, but he's also incredibly handsome. Those blue eyes make your knees weak!

Most people are familiar with "Rumsfeld's Rules," the constantly updated list of the way Secretary Rumsfeld views life and the rules that govern it. By now, you know I like people who speak bluntly and use their common sense. Secretary Rumsfeld, of course, is a paragon of straight talk. Why does he feel confident speaking his mind so freely? What influenced the man who is directing war operations and the biggest military in history? I'd wanted to know for a long time, so I asked him.

EXPECT THAT NOT EVERYBODY WILL LIKE EVERYTHING YOU DO

From one or both of my parents I inherited a joy of reading, and I spent a great deal of my time reading history and biographies. If you read about George Washington, John Adams, or Lincoln, or Truman, or Roosevelt, you can't help but be amazed by the criticism and harshness they endured. Truman may have gone out of office with a 25 percent positive rating, but he was an impressive president when you look at what he accomplished. I remember being in a courtyard in Coronado, California, when President Roosevelt died. A lot of kids cheered! Remember, this was before the end of World War II. I was stunned. These were all people who were doing great things, and they were criticized.

One of my entries in Rumsfeld's Rules says, "If you do something, somebody is not going to like it. Conversely, if you don't do anything, that won't happen." And, it's true. I've come to expect that somebody won't like everything I do. I'm okay with that.

IF AMERICA STUMBLES, THE WORLD FALLS

When I think about the advice that changed my life, I remember a speech Adlai Stevenson gave to my senior class at Princeton in 1954. Stevenson said, "If those young Americans who have the advantage of education, perspective, and self-discipline do not participate to the fullest extent of their ability, America will stumble, and if America stumbles the world falls." He inspired us to be engaged, involved, and to recognize that government merits our attention as citizens. It was one of the best speeches I've ever heard, and it hit me at just the right point in my life.

Later in the speech, Stevenson said, "Our American government may be defined, perhaps, as the government that really cares about the people. Just so, our government demands, it depends upon, the care and the devotion of the people. I would suggest to you, then, that it is the duty of an educated man in America today to work actively to put good men into public office— and to defend them there against abuse and the ugly inclination we, as human beings, have to believe the worst." This guy lost two presidential races in a row, and yet he had this wonderful perspective on the role of our country and the role of our citizenry.

LEAD BY PERSUASION

Serving my country was something that was natural for me. I'd been in the ROTC during college. My father was in the navy, and I went into the navy, too. While I always knew there was some extent of public service in my future, that speech was the inspiration that steered me toward public service in an even broader way. I went to Washington after I got out of the navy in 1957 because a congressman I'd met gave me a job. By 1962, I decided I wanted to run for Congress myself. It's the one public service job I really pursued, because I wanted it so deeply. I won and stayed in Congress until 1969, when I resigned to become an assistant to President Nixon. By 1971,

I was counselor to the president. I left in 1973 to become the U.S. Ambassador to NATO. I was soon called back when President Nixon resigned, and I became chief of staff for President Gerald Ford.

That was the worst job I ever had. It was just a tough time for the country. It was an ugly period. You shouldn't weaken the government by commanding people to do things. You lead by persuasion, and you can't persuade people if they don't trust you. The reservoir of trust had been drained dry. People in the Ford administration had to function within an institution that had been deemed to be illegitimate or unacceptable by the American people. Imagine walking out and saying something like, "That is a ceiling," and having people think that, because you're saying it is a ceiling, maybe it's not; maybe there's a hidden reason you're saying it is. It was a tough time.

I left government when President Ford lost and went into business, but I stayed involved as a Middle East envoy and other various things. I was amazed when I was asked to come back here. I feel very fortunate to be able to be a public servant.

TRY TO WORK WITH PEOPLE
SMARTER THAN YOU ARE

I'm not sure where my personality came from. I like people and I like talking to people, engaging them in subjects and being around them, because no one is smart enough to know how to do this job alone. As Stevenson noted in his speech, even back in 1954 the United States government had 155,000 governing units, one million elected officials, and six million full-time employees. The government is vastly larger now. So unless you're a Mozart or an Einstein, and you can go off by yourself and do something brilliant, which most of us can't, you need to bring in other people.

As a management approach, I try to work with people who are smarter than I am. I find people whose experiences are different from mine, who preferably have a sense of humor so I don't mind spending long hours with them, and then get them to talk openly about how they'd approach some issue, because I can't divine it. Always remember that you are not smarter than everybody else. Even if you have more experience than most people do in some area, even if you know more about something, you don't know more about everything. You just have to face that, find ways to get others to contribute their insights, and bring all those things together into a rational approach for the country, or company, or department you're serving.

PEOPLE DESERVE A DIRECT ANSWER

I'm from the Midwest, not from this part of the world, and I think my tendency to give you a direct answer if you ask me a direct question is a characteristic of the region. I've been around Washington for a good while and I try to remain very accessible because I believe it's enormously important for people to understand this institution. I'll talk to people and say what I think and I don't have to hedge anything. I'm not worried about next week or next month. I think people deserve a fairly direct answer and so I try to give it.

I remember the mistrust after the Nixon administration. Maybe that's the reason for my directness. You have to have principles, and they have to be straightforward and, to the extent humanly possible, not debatable. Obviously, that's the best policy in a country where people are governed through representatives. They are owed the truth. I think this evening I'll add that to Rumsfeld's Rules.

PATRICIA F. RUSSO
CEO, LUCENT TECHNOLOGIES

Despite the rise of power among females in the workplace, it is still relatively rare to see a woman become CEO of one of the most powerful companies in the world. Pat Russo, CEO of Lucent Technologies, is highly admired and respected by her peers. She received her undergraduate degree from Georgetown and completed the Advanced Management Program at Harvard University. She has an Honorary Doctorate of Engineering from Stevens Institute of Technology and an Honorary Doctorate in Entrepreneurial Studies from Columbia College. She helped launch Lucent in 1996, became its CEO in 2002, and has since led Lucent's return to profitability during one of the most challenging periods in the telecom industry's history. She has also served as president of Eastman Kodak. She is a gifted business leader.

NEVER FEEL CONSTRAINED ABOUT WHAT YOU CAN DO WITH YOUR LIFE

My parents were both very powerful influences on my life. I distinctly remember my father always telling me as a young kid that, when I thought about my life, I should realize that I could do anything I wanted to do. So, very early on, I knew I should never feel constrained about my options for the future. That was rare advice at the time, because in those days girls generally had very few professional opportunities to look forward to. Today, it's a very different world.

UNDERSTAND THE DIFFERENCE BETWEEN TRAGEDY AND INCONVENIENCE

My mother taught me that attitude is very important to everything you do. Here was a woman who had seven children in eight years, two of them disabled twins. One has been in a wheelchair his entire life and has gone through multiple surgeries. The other is deaf and has neurological issues. Both still live with her and need to be cared for nonstop. My father died at a relatively young age. Yet, despite all of this, she considers herself the most blessed person in the world. She's never complained in my entire life. She wakes up with an *I-am-just-so-blessed* attitude. When people ask her how she does it, she says, "You just do it." It's a matter of fact.

Her example has really taught me a lot about understanding the difference between what's a tragedy and what's really just an inconvenience. One of my brothers is the happiest person you'll ever meet in your life, yet he has these physical challenges. I saw a T-shirt once that said, "Attitude is contagious. Is yours worth catching?" With my experience, I could only say to myself, "How true that is."

CREATE A SENSE OF POSSIBILITY

My daughter-in-law is a terrific mother. While some parents constantly point out what their children are doing wrong, she continually tells her kids, "You can do it. You can do it." Consider the formative impressions that those words have on little human beings. I believe that the most important part of helping children (and businesses for that matter) fulfill their potential is creating a sense of possibility. Attitude has a lot to do with that.

WHAT GOT YOU HERE MAY NOT GET YOU ANY FURTHER

In my business life, one piece of advice has really stuck with me. When I was working for AT&T, I was promoted to a fairly high-level position. One of the guys, whom I respected for his wisdom, told me, "It's important for you to remember, as you proceed in your business career, that what has gotten you this far won't necessarily get you further. Every step along the way, you've got to stop and reflect about what you need to do differently, given a differing set of responsibilities." That was very helpful to me. The power of that advice was that it made me conscious of being able to make distinctions.

Think about what you carry forward, in terms of how you work, and what you do, and what you need to change. It's important to ask yourself: What set of skills will work for me in a new environment?

TRUST YOUR INSTINCTS

The other thing I've learned—and I'm not sure if it's been as much advice as it is something I've just learned over and over again—is to trust my instincts. I've come to believe that the word "instinct" doesn't do justice to the value that it really has. Most people think "instinct" simply refers to a quick reaction, but instinct really encapsulates your years of experience and what they tell you. I think we need to think of instinct that way, rather than dismiss it as something offhand. When dealing with complex business issues, I tell people to trust their instincts—and by that I mean that they should trust their life experiences, the good and the bad, what they've done well and what they've not. All of those experiences are speaking to you. There have been times when I've been hesitant about doing something, but I've learned that trusting my instincts and being roughly right is often good enough.

In other words, don't give up the good in pursuit of the perfect.

Jim Ryun breaking a world record, 1965

JIM RYUN

UNITED STATES CONGRESSMAN AND THREE-TIME OLYMPIAN

★ ★ ★

Imagine a high school senior winning against an Olympic champion at a track meet. Well, Jim Ryun did just that. Running a 3:55.3 mile, he beat Peter Snell in 1965—transforming Ryun from high school star to international sensation. That record stood for more than thirty-five years. Despite struggling with exercise-induced asthma, Jim Ryun was heralded as the youngest Sportsman of the Year in the history of Sports Illustrated. *He is a three-time Olympian, has held three world records in three different events, and has held the record for being the fastest man in the world.*

Sometimes, when people achieve success so early in life, they try to rest on their laurels for the rest of their lives. In contrast, Jim Ryun uses his own success story to try to help other people. Before serving in Congress, he helped create Sounds of Success, an organization that helps hearing-impaired children fulfill their potential. He is the founder of Jim Ryun Sports Inc., a public relations company that promotes various charities.

While I was aware of Representative Ryun's sports success, what struck me most about him is his commitment to his family. He has four adult children: Heather, Ned, Drew, and Catharine. Recently, I bumped into them out bowling together, and clearly they were having a wonderful time.

STEP OFF THE PEDESTAL

My life changed when my wife, Anne, and I became Christians on May 18, 1972. Clara and Bernie Taylor, an older couple we knew, inspired us with their strong relationship with each other and with God. Bernie was one of the football coaches at the University of Kansas, and he and Clara both had a certain serenity about them. They seemed to have achieved a greater sense of peace and direction as a result of their relationship with Christ. They told us that Jesus gave them a feeling of satisfaction that they had never realized through their involvement in athletics, or anything else for that matter. They told us that we should bring Christ into our lives, and Anne and I realized that we wanted what they had.

We had many wonderful conversations with Bernie and Clara, and one night we prayed and asked Christ to come into our lives. Accepting Christ transformed us in a very subtle yet dramatic way. As an athlete, I was used to getting attention and believing that the world revolved around me. My relationship with God allowed me to step off my pedestal, and it also gave me a sense of purpose that would last for years to come.

LEARN TO FORGIVE YOURSELF

Before the Munich Olympics in 1972, I was the favorite to win the gold medal. At the beginning of the games, I had no idea just how important my commitment to becoming a Christian and trusting in Christ would be. In Munich, during the 1,500-meter race, I tripped and failed to reach the finals. When I fell, Anne got out of the stands and came to find me. This was no small feat, because security was tight due to the Black September group terrorist activity and the massacre at the Munich airport. Somehow she got through and we embraced each other and began to pray.

We spent the next day trying to figure out what to do. It seemed my entire Olympic delegation had abandoned me. In the end, we turned to sportscaster Howard Cosell for help. He helped me write a petition for reinstatement to the games. While I was not reinstated, the experience ended up being something of a personal triumph because I learned how to understand and deal with failure. Up to that point, I'd only experienced great success. After Munich, I had to learn how to forgive myself for falling.

Forgiveness and understanding became the blueprint for my future as I entered politics and as we raised our children. Back in 1972, the success I had known as a young man disappeared—but my faith allowed me to move on from athletics and achieve everything else I ever wanted.

GIVE BACK TO OUR COUNTRY

In the spring of 1996, I carried the Olympic torch across Kansas. At a ceremony in Wichita, Representative Tiahrt turned to me and said, "Jim, you know, Representative Brownback has just stepped down from his seat in the second district. You should consider running for the seat." As Anne and I drove back to Lawrence, I turned to her and said, "Honey, we've always talked about wanting to help shape the direction of our country. Maybe this is our turn to step up and be part of something." She later told me she almost fell out of the car from shock.

We went home and I told the children. We said this was something we wanted them to pray about, because we needed to make a quick decision. After a couple of days we entered the race, knowing that it would change our lives. The kids jumped right in to help campaign. They went out in pairs, while Anne and I went out together. Drew and Heather, Ned and Catherine, and Anne and I covered the twenty counties in the eastern part of Kansas in no time.

My time in Congress has given us an opportunity to give back to our country. When I was an athlete, I traveled to the old Soviet Union and the socialist countries, and I would always came back appreciating America. I always hoped that someday I would have an opportunity to step into leadership and help make my own country even better. My relationship with Christ helped me put down moral foundations that have endured the challenges of politics. When you come to Washington, you realize that part of the art of politics is compromise. However, for me, there are certain issues— those that deal with people's lives and well-being—on which I will not compromise.

BE CLOSER TO HOME

As a husband and a father, I know I'm entrusted with five precious lives. As my four children grew up, I always wanted to make sure that I was around to help raise them and instill in them the values and principles that Anne and I cherish. Instead of wanting to make more money, I've always wanted to be closer to home. I remember a reporter one time asked me how becoming a Christian has changed my life in the political arena. I said, "It's taught me how to serve people. This is a position for serving people. I think it's a tremendous honor to do that."

Connie Sellecca and her son, Gib

CONNIE SELLECCA

ACTRESS

★ ★ ★

Connie Sellecca is one of the most beautiful women you will ever meet. She began her acting career in New York, where she was already a successful model. The television series The Greatest American Hero *brought her to the attention of many viewers, but it was her role on the extremely popular series* Hotel *that made her famous. Since 1980 she's made an average of a movie a year. So many women admired her sense of personal style that Montgomery Ward began selling Connie's own clothing and accessories line. She later created her own all-natural-ingredient skin care line, the Sellecca Solution, based on an Egyptian cream she found during her travels. Her own wrinkle-free and flawless skin convinces me that it works!*

However, Connie's beauty extends well beyond the surface. When the tsunami devastated Southeast Asia, she packed up her family's bags and they all traveled to Sri Lanka to assist Operation Blessing's relief effort in the fishing villages of the Ampara district. While working in the relief camps, Connie's family helped the children express their feelings through crayon drawings. The images the children produced were so moving that Connie and her family published a book, Shades of Blue, *from which profits are being donated to a relief and rebuilding program.*

THE HARD ROAD WILL ALWAYS BE THE RIGHT ROAD

Around the time when I was going through my divorce, I met a man named Coleman Luck. It was a very difficult time for me, and he really helped me keep it together. We met through my church, and I remember him saying, "When you come to a crossroad in life, you can either take the easy road or the hard road. The hard road will always be the right road." I've looked at everything that way ever since, and I agree with him wholeheartedly. I did take a hard road, and I couldn't imagine ever ending up in such a wonderful place. Now, I give the same advice to my children.

GROW STRONGER FROM PAIN AND EXPERIENCE

My father died during the divorce; in essence, I lost the two men I had always relied on. Some people might have sat in a chair taking antidepressants and let life pass them by, but I didn't. I made the choice to grow stronger from the pain I was experiencing. It would have been easy to grow bitter and to blame my ex-husband for everything that went wrong. But I chose to take the hard road, not to blame him and resent him, but to move on.

I was a single mom for a very long time, and had to learn to balance work and family. I had to figure out how to raise my son, Gib, while also working full time. Somehow, it always worked out. Whenever Gib was sick, I managed to stay home with him and get him to the doctor. I was determined to be with him whenever he needed me. It was rough, because the entertainment industry is so competitive, and there's always someone else ready to take your job. But taking the hard road ended up working out in the end.

THE DIFFICULT ROAD LEADS TO INCREDIBLE REWARDS

Working became more difficult when I had my second child. The television industry had changed quite a bit. Hollywood used to be the center of the TV universe. Now there are satellite Hollywoods in Minneapolis, Atlanta, Austin, North Carolina, and up in Canada. My daughter is still in school, and as any parent knows, you just can't pull them out to go from job to job with you. When she started kindergarten, I had to start making decisions that were very difficult. While I've made many mistakes in my career, I know I've made the right choices as a parent. Now I have an incredible husband and a life I couldn't even imagine before. Trust me, the more difficult road always leads to incredible rewards.

HANNAH STORM

TELEVISION SPORTSCASTER AND HOST

★ ★ ★

Hannah Storm grew up in a sports household. Her father was commissioner of the ABA and the president of the NBA's Atlanta Hawks. After struggling to get into sportscasting, Hannah paved the way for other women. In 1988, after broadcasting sports on the radio, she landed a job at CNN, after an interview in which she had to take a sports quiz that none of the male applicants were asked to take. There she anchored CNN Sports Tonight *and other shows. NBC hired her in 1992, and after two years she was named the primary sideline reporter for NFL coverage. A year later, Hannah became the first woman to host a weekly network pregame show for a major sport.*

USING YOUR SPECIFIC TALENTS IS AN INCREDIBLY IMPORTANT THING TO DO

When I graduated from the University of Notre Dame in 1983, I became a radio DJ with dreams of eventually becoming a sportscaster broadcasting the Olympics and a morning show. It's amazing that it all actually ended up happening, but I guess that's the power of visualization.

I became a radio DJ because no one would hire a woman as a sports-caster. About two years after college, I returned to Notre Dame for my brother's graduation. We were in the basement of a dorm at a graduation party when I ran into Father Mark Porman, a priest I'd become friendly with when I was an undergrad. I told him that being back on such a spiritual campus made me realize that I was having second thoughts about the direction of my life. I'd grown up doing a lot of charity work. After graduation, my brother was going to help war refugees in Cambodia. I began to question whether what I was doing was meaningful. I know I was following my own dreams, but I wasn't sure I was really making the world a better place.

In our conversation, Father Mark told me two things. First of all, he said, "God gives each of us specific talents, and using those to the best of our abilities is an incredibly important thing to do." Second, he told me, "In your career you can make a difference on several levels, by the way you conduct yourself in a very competitive arena and how you treat people as you're trying to get ahead."

I see the truth in that advice. Being on the radio or TV gives me the chance to do a lot of good. Even if you're just broadcasting sports, you're taking people away from the troubles of their life and helping them enjoy their day. While reading the news, you're informing people and also sharing their stories of both inspiration and heartache. Father Mark taught me to see my life as a chance to make the world a better place after all—by being a good example for others.

YOU JUST NEED ONE PERSON TO SAY YES

When I graduated from college, I really wanted to work in sports. But I couldn't get a job. Time and time again, I heard the same thing from news directors: "I can't hire a woman." "It's too risky to hire a woman." "I'll hire a woman over my dead body."

But my dad was fantastic, because he's a glass-is-half-full kind of guy. He's very, very positive. He told me to take any on-air job I could find. So, after answering a want ad in the back of a broadcasting magazine, I got the job as a DJ. Then my dad told me, "Always remember, Hannah Lynn, no matter how many people say no, all you need to find is one single person to say yes. Just one person." All it takes is that one person who sees your potential. That makes it easier to live with all the rejections. Rather than become bitter and dejected, I've always forged straight ahead pursuing my dreams. To paraphrase Tommy Lasorda: "Don't look at all the doors that are closed, look at the one window that's open."

JOHN TESH

TELEVISION AND RADIO JOURNALIST
AND MUSICIAN

★ ★ ★

It's hard to imagine John Tesh dressed as a Klingon warrior, but that's exactly what he did, for an episode of one of his favorite TV shows, Star Trek: The Next Generation*! It just goes to show how versatile this renaissance man really is.*

Most people are familiar with John from his ten years as host of Entertainment Tonight. *Many were shocked when he left that lucrative, high-profile position. But then again John's always been hard to classify. He has won six Emmys and an AP award for investigative journalism, and has worked as an announcer during the Olympic Games. However, his true passion is music. Three of John's albums have gone gold, he's had several number one radio hits on both the Christian and pop charts, and he has received two Grammy nominations. His Christianity speaks to you but doesn't shout at you. Through worship music, John now connects with people in a much deeper and more personal way than he ever could before. His radio show,* Intelligence for Your Life, *is on the air across the nation, blending soft rock with John's thoughts and interesting news tidbits. I personally love his television special* Live at Red Rocks, *which was one of PBS's most successful fund-raising specials ever. He says his goal in life is simply to be useful to others.*

BE HONEST ABOUT YOUR FAITH

I'd been married for two years when I went to this huge meeting of a group called the Promise Keepers. It was held in the L.A. Coliseum and there were about eighty thousand men in attendance. For a moment, I thought, "What have I gotten myself into?" I was looking around me, and it all just seemed way too "manly." Honestly, that's the only way to describe it. At this meeting, you learn tools to become a better husband, and, in my case, a better stepparent. Dr. Tom Evans, who was leading the event, got up on stage and started really yelling at us. "You Christian men here in Los Angeles," he said, "you've been given God's blessing every single day, but you're closet Christians. You're in the closet with the door shut and light off. How dare you closet Christians not go public for God? There you are accepting God's blessing. It's time to come out."

That moment was transformative for me. I sort of jumped out of my seat and realized that it was time for me to be honest about my faith. I'd been working on *Entertainment Tonight*, and it was really difficult. I'd been refusing to say stupid things like "stud muffin" on the air, and they'd started to ask, "Are you a Christian?" Now this caused a real conflict for me. Here I was doing this show Monday to Friday and going to church on Sunday. I didn't feel comfortable. The moment Dr. Evans said, "You shouldn't be closet Christians. You should go public for God," I really started setting new goals. I decided to spend more time with the Scripture.

ASK YOURSELF WHAT IT IS THAT MAKES YOU FULLY COME ALIVE, AND GO DO THAT

I read a book called *Wild at Heart*. The best piece of advice was a quote from Frederick Beekman that said, "When you're trying to figure out your goal, don't ask yourself what the world needs, ask yourself what it is that makes you come fully alive, and go do that. Because God wants men and women who are fully alive." I also listen to Rick Warren's *Purpose-Driven Life* on my iPod. His book discusses setting a goal and then surrounding it with Scripture. I think that hard work, risk taking, and prayer are the three most important components of your life. You have to work hard, but if the work isn't what you were meant to be doing, you have to take the risk of walking away from it. And, if you continue to pray for guidance, you'll be fine.

TAKE A STEP OF FAITH AND WALK AWAY

I'd been working on *Entertainment Tonight* for ten years. I'd get about five letters a week, usually from people wanting me to get Phil Collins's autograph for them. I didn't feel useful. I had a big job, a seven-figure salary, a number one record, and a beautiful wife. But then I started to get fan letters about my music. One man said he had listened to one of my songs during his son's surgery. At that point, it hit me that music was how I could make a difference in people's lives. I want to speak to people's hearts and be useful to them. I had to take a step of faith and walk away from my *ET* job to start doing a job that made a difference.

THINK ABOUT THE HYPHEN IN YOUR LIFE

Do you ever get concerned about the hyphen in your life? It's the period between the start date and end date on your tombstone. My whole family has begun to evolve. We went to Sri Lanka after the tsunami because we saw people who needed help. We were just doing what our family does; the only thing different was the country we were in. Serving people, in any ways we can, is the goal of our lives now. Before, I had everything. At least that's what I thought. But I didn't have a relationship with God that was honoring Him. That advice from Dr. Evans in the coliseum gave me the inspiration to take the steps toward what I now know is my true life.

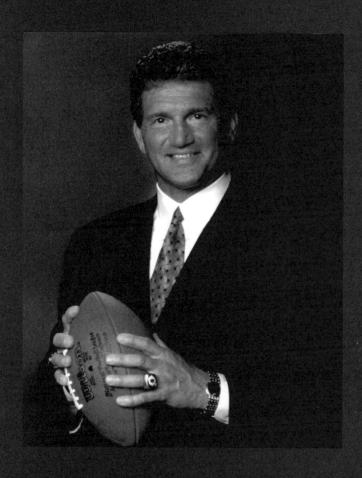

JOE THEISMANN

SPORTSCASTER AND RETIRED
NFL FOOTBALL PLAYER

★ ★ ★

Whenever I want to encourage my boys in sports, I use Joe Theismann as an example. Everyone thought he was too small to be a great football player, and he proved them all wrong in a big way. Joe led the Washington Redskins to victory in Super Bowl XVII, was named the Pro Bowl Player of the Game in 1982 and 1983, was voted onto the UPI All-NFC team, and was named the NFL Most Valuable Player by the AP.

Yet Joe's attitude grew with his fame. Today he's the first person to admit it, but the Joe Thiesmann of today is a very different man from what he was like twenty years ago. He still works hard, as a successful ESPN football analyst, but off-screen he's changed. Joe takes time for people. He's still gregarious, but it's in a comfortable, friendly way. Joe is now a friend to many, not just the star of his own one-man show.

DON'T EVER LET YOUR DREAMS DIE

I was a very skinny kid. I graduated from high school weighing 148 pounds. My mom knew I wanted to play ball; she knew that was what I really loved. I certainly loved playing sports much more than I enjoyed school!

At 148 pounds, people used to tell me I was too small to be serious about sports. From my days playing Pop Warner football, though, my mother gave me much better advice. "Don't ever let anybody tell you that you can't have what you want," she said. "Don't ever let your dreams die." Whenever I had doubts about pursuing my dream, I would remember her words.

BE THE BEST BECAUSE *YOU* WANT TO BE

They said I couldn't and shouldn't play at the University of Notre Dame because I'd be going up against thirteen other quarterbacks. But I kept a sign on my desk that read, "I want to be the best quarterback to ever play at Notre Dame." They'd say, "This is the greatest football program in history, and you want to be the best? Come on." Well, I never got to the *"Come on"* part. I just assumed I'd be the best because I wanted to be.

Later, they said I shouldn't go into professional football. I was in Philadelphia the day of the NFL draft. Pete Retzlaff, the general manager of the Philadelphia Eagles, came up to me right before the picks. He looked at me and asked, "How tall are you?" and I said, "I'm about six feet." He replied, "You look five-ten." Then he asked me, "How much do you weigh?" and I said, "Oh, about 180 pounds." And he shot back, "Well, you look 165." Then he turned and walked away. I remember thinking, "I'm not being drafted by the Eagles." And I wasn't, because he thought I was too small.

Then, once I was in professional football, people said my arm wasn't strong enough, and that mobile quarterbacks like me can't win championships. People kept telling me why I shouldn't be going where I wanted to go. By then, I'd learned that when other people start telling you you can't do something, you should try to figure out what their motivations might be. It could be that they want you to fail, or that they're jealous of your talents. It could also be that they just don't believe in you. I have no idea where I'd be today if I'd listened to all those people who told me I couldn't make it in football.

DON'T LET SUCCESS TURN YOU INTO A JERK

My mom's words inspired me in the early part of my life, but it was only after I broke my leg that I understood their deeper meaning. I'd let my early success turn me into a jerk. Really, I wasn't a nice person. My athletic ability was my ticket to money, popularity, and everything else you could dream of. Then it was taken away, in a sack most football fans will never forget. I certainly won't; it changed my life. I'd led the Redskins to the Super Bowl two years in a row.

Then, during a Monday night game against the Giants, an LT tackled me. My leg snapped, and in a second the world that I loved so much was taken away.

After my injury, I had to learn how to be a normal person. But I wasn't a nice person. I had fallen into the trap of feeling special. I had alienated my friends. So I had to start over—as a person and as a professional. As I began down the road of rehabilitation, I kept in mind my mother's words. I was still determined to keep my dreams alive, but I needed a new dream.

BE OPEN TO NEW DREAMS

After the Super Bowl XVII win in 1982, I had the opportunity to do a lot of public speaking. I really enjoyed getting up and talking to groups of people. Still, I was shocked in January 1985 when ABC approached me about a job. O. J. Simpson, Frank Gifford, and Don Meredith had been hosting *Monday Night Football,* and ABC had the Super Bowl that year. They really wanted Howard Cosell to come back to Monday night television, but he turned them down. So they came to me after the season was over and said, "We'd like you to participate in the Super Bowl." I didn't really believe them, but they came back and said, "We want you to replace O. J. in the booth with Frank and Dan." I couldn't believe the opportunity. But I also realized that it would be a tough pass–fail test. I was going to broadcast the Super Bowl without any experience, practice, or training. Luckily, the night went well, and I knew I'd found my new dream. That Super Bowl show led to my job at ESPN, where I've been for seventeen years.

WHY LIMIT YOURSELF?

I prepare just as much for a broadcast as I did for a game. I don't want to be just another announcer. I want to teach people professional football. When people watch the game, I want them to turn to someone in their living room or at a bar stool next to them and say, "I learned something about football today." When I talk to teams, I ask them this: "Why can't you be the winner? Why does it have to be the other guy? Why limit yourself?" I tell them, "Don't ever let anyone tell you that you can't win a championship, or that you can't make a difference in someone's life. Don't let people dictate to you what your life is going to be."

YOU CONTROL WHERE YOU GO—NO EXCUSES

As I've grown older, I realize that I want to be the sort of person who can make a commitment and keep his word. Too often, people have a litany of excuses that they can't do something. "Well, I got a bad break when I was a kid," they'll say. "I wasn't able to do this or that." It's convenient to succumb to pressures and get dragged down by negative situations. My mom cut off those kinds of excuses right from the start. What I learned is that you control where you go. When I give speeches, I tell people, "I had a choice whether to come here today, and I came. I care about every one of you in this room."

INFLUENCE SOMEONE ELSE . . . THE ADVICE IS THE ONE CONSTANT

I'm shocked sometimes when I look back at what I've accomplished. I pinch myself. You know, I don't think I ever told many people that we put a clause in my contract in the early 1980s that if I were the league MVP I'd get fifty thousand dollars. At the time, I was the third-string quarterback. Heck, I was a punt returner. What were the chances of my accomplishing that goal? All of a sudden, in 1983 I was MVP . . . and fifty thousand dollars richer!

It's hard to explain how I felt when I had to walk off the football field on January 31, 1983. At the time, I felt like I'd reached the top of the mountain. Now I realize that I still had a long way to go. I continue to climb. It's my job to take responsibility for my life and see if I can influence or help someone else. For me, thinking about the impact of my mom's advice is like connecting the dots of my life. You'll be at a decision point in your life, and *bang!* there comes that dot again. Someday, when I'm laid to rest, I'll have had a lifetime of fulfillment—all because of a few words my mom shared with me a long time ago. It wasn't until talking to you, E. D., that I realized I've never told my mom how important those words of advice were. I'm going to see her this week and let her know.

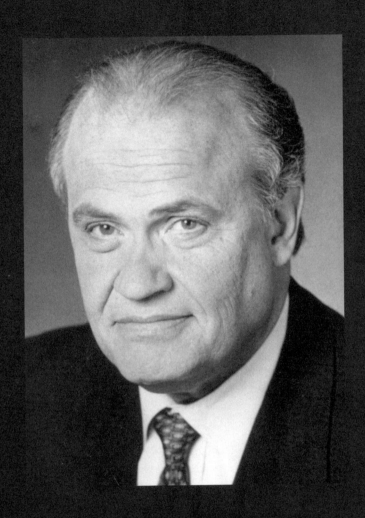

FRED THOMPSON

UNITED STATES SENATOR AND ACTOR

★ ★ ★

Fred Thompson is an unlikely actor, and he'll tell you as much himself. He doesn't carry himself like a Hollywood heavyweight; he doesn't talk much about the industry, and he found success by coincidence. Fred was terrific in a number of movies, including The Hunt for Red October, *and currently stars on the hit television series* Law & Order. *Fred became a senator rather unexpectedly as well. He was elected to fill in for Al Gore, who left to run for vice president. After two years in Washington, Fred jokes, he often longs for the realism and sincerity of Hollywood!*

Whether he's shooting a movie in Hollywood or discussing the issues in D.C., Fred makes an impression on you. He's a determined man, and he sets his own rules.

HE SET AN EXAMPLE WITH HIS LIFE

My dad survived the Depression, and as I look back on it, he had a rough time. He almost starved to death, and he was pretty rough in every respect. He sold used cars in the small town of Lawrenceburg, Tennessee. He had an eighth-grade education. When I got married at the age of seventeen and left home, he quit giving me advice and treated me like a man.

Still, his example was far more powerful than any words of advice he could have given me. My father worked very hard, but every day at 6 P.M. he was home. He was a good provider, and I never heard him raise his voice at my mother. He made me feel like the most secure guy in the world; I always thought that he could do anything.

CONFIDENCE AND AMBITION COME FROM A SUPPORTIVE FAMILY

Whenever an opportunity comes along, I know within the first ten seconds whether or not it's something I'm interested in. I think that having such a supportive family has always given me confidence and ambition. My mom and dad were proud when I graduated from high school. Then I went on to graduate from Memphis State University and I got my J.D. from Vanderbilt. It never occurred to me that I couldn't do whatever I wanted to do.

I went back to Lawrenceburg and practiced law for two years. After that I had the chance to go to Nashville and become assistant U.S. attorney in 1969. The dean of the bar down in Lawrenceburg took me aside and said, "You really shouldn't do that. You should stay here and build your practice. You can become a leading attorney here in Lawrenceburg." I'm pretty bullheaded. I didn't listen to him and went to Nashville.

Later on, just as I was beginning to establish my own law practice, Watergate came along, and I was offered a position on the committee. Some people told me not to take the position, because it would take away time from my practice. But the opportunity sounded exciting, so I took it, and became co-chief counsel to the Senate Watergate Committee. On that committee, I had a chance to work side-by-side with Howard Baker. I asked Baker specifically how to handle things because we had a tiger by the tail. He just said, "You're a good lawyer. You've got good instincts; use them and I'm sure you'll do fine." That's the only advice he ever gave me. But I learned as I sat there and I watched Howard. He was always calm. I never saw him lose his temper. I never saw him say anything really harsh or mean about anybody. I saw him maintain his composure, and so I sat there and held my own tongue, and I came out at the end much better for it.

TAKE IT ON

One time, I decided to take a case that had very little upside in political or monetary terms. A young woman came to me and said she was being taken advantage of. She told me, "I watched you in the Watergate hearings and thought that if I ever got in trouble I'd come to see you. Well, I'm in trouble. I'm the chairman of the parole board, and they're about to fire me. I'm very suspicious of some things that are going on, and I don't like what they're doing." Sure enough, Governor Ray Blanton called a press conference and fired her and embarrassed her. I thought, "What the hell? I'm taking this on." Well, that case eventually helped take down the governor on charges of selling pardons.

A book was written about the Governor Blanton case, and when they came to town to film it, there I was. One thing led to another, and they asked me if I wanted to play myself. I said, "Why not?" If I failed, I figured, so what? All they could do was send me home, and I'd go back to what I was doing. I had nothing at stake really, except hurt feelings maybe. And in the process I discovered that I have a knack for acting. I have a friend who took up painting in her forties, and discovered she was a wonderful painter. Others have done the same with music. I realized that I could ignore the camera and act natural in unnatural circumstances. That was all it took.

DON'T WASTE YOUR TIME ASKING FOR ADVICE

After a couple of movies, I decided to run for Al Gore's senate seat when he ran for vice president. I've always gotten a kick out of the advice I got from a friend of mine who was a politician in Missouri. He was running for judge in his town. Like many politicians in Missouri, he visited President Truman, who was quite elderly at the time. He said, "Mr. President, I'm here to ask you what advice you have to offer me as I run for this position." And the president replied, "My advice, young man, is to not waste your time going around asking for advice from people like me." That's pretty much the advice I've followed throughout my life.

Jonathan Tisch and his father, Bob

JONATHAN TISCH

CEO OF LOEWS CORPORATION

The first time I met Jonathan Tisch, we were both sitting on one of those tiny benches you find in the hallways outside preschool classrooms—you know, the ones you worry will crack under the weight of an adult. This classroom also had a small cubbyhole with a two-way mirror, so you could check in to see how your child was managing the change from being with mommy and daddy to being a student. We've all experienced that sinking feeling when we find out they can be just fine without you holding their hand!

I saw Jon often at the school, dropping off and picking up his kids, and expressing great pride after viewing their finger-painted artwork! That's the image of Jon I have in my head. But I've come to see his other side. Jon is one of the most determined and focused people I've ever met. If something needs to get done and Jon says he'll do it, you don't have to think about it again. He loves New York City, and works endlessly to promote tourism. Jon is the ultimate New Yorker. He works at warp speed, and effortlessly handles his job as chairman and CEO of Loews Corporation while chairing the local convention and visitors bureau and working on the council for rebuilding lower Manhattan. Crain's magazine named him one of the nation's top ten most influential business leaders. Jon also serves on the board of the Elizabeth Glaser Pediatric AIDS Foundation, Tufts University, the Tribeca Film Institute, and the New York Giants.

IT'S ABOUT "WE"

My first boss taught me a lesson I still focus on today. He told me, "Never start a paragraph with the word 'I.'" In those days we were still writing letters; these days we're more likely to write e-mails. If you look at a letter and go down the left column and you see a lot of "I's," that's a sign that the person writing thinks of himself as more important than you. It's a fascinating thing to think about: it's not about "I," it's about "we." I wrote a book inspired by that advice, called *The Power of We*. I'm grateful to have learned, early on, that I needed to create situations where I could craft success for both my own company and for others. Understanding that it's not all about you can help you create situations where it's about "we."

CREATE SUCCESS FOR OTHERS

In business, I also believe it's important to negotiate in such a way that both sides come out looking great. You should be concerned about the person you're working with, so that you can create a win-win situation. A success for both sides is a success for you. Creating that kind of win-win partnership has served Loews Hotel Corporation very well. When we build a hotel, the corporation certainly benefits, but the community you've built in also wins, because the new hotel creates new jobs. It's important to be a good neighbor.

LOOK FORWARD

If you're doing things for the right reasons, you don't need to look back. Make decisions based on the information you have in front of you. Keep in mind that sometimes things won't turn out the way you want them to; still, you have to look forward.

These life lessons have had a great impact on how I run the Loews Hotel Corporation. We have only twenty properties. We're fairly small in today's landscape of mega-giants—like the Marriotts, with 2,600 hotels, or the Hiltons, with 2,200. Yet it's amazing to see how often people assume we're much larger than we are because of our ability to go out into the community and generate positive press through our creative marketing initiatives. Loews is a family business, and I'm lucky to have the opportunity to incorporate what I learned from my late father and uncle into the way my two cousins and I run the company today.

LET PEOPLE PUT THEIR TRUST IN YOU

The entire hotel industry has changed greatly. There's the hotel business, and then there's the business of hotels. The business of hotels is what is changing dramatically. The industry has matured; today, it is very sophisticated and highly competitive. However, one thing has not changed, and that's the notion of hospitality, which has been around for thousands of years. When a family leaves their home and the safety and security of their own environment and comes to you, for whatever reason, they're putting their trust in you, to make them feel comfortable and to keep them safe.

TREAT EVERYONE WITH RESPECT

Too often, I have noticed, people are taken for granted and not treated with respect. In our business you have to treat everyone with respect, no matter what. And I believe the same goes for any other business you want to succeed in. Whether you work for a private-sector company or in the pro bono world, you have to treat people with respect. You have to understand that people have something to say, and that you have the ability to listen to them, to be gracious, and say thank you.

In today's world, businesses are incredibly competitive. There are too many good, smart, well-capitalized companies and individuals who can do what you do, and sometimes they can do it better. There's always some other guy behind you who's working a little harder. That's why it's important to look at your clients and thank them regularly. The same goes for your staff, whether it's the upper echelon in senior management or, in my case, the housekeepers and members of the bell staff or waiters and waitresses. You have to respect them and say thank you. Sometimes smart people make mistakes because they take people for granted and don't have the humility or courtesy to say, "Thank you. I appreciate what you do for me."

I hope never to make that mistake.

Donald Trump at the New York Military Academy with his parents, 1964

DONALD TRUMP

REAL ESTATE DEVELOPER

★ ★ ★

I now adore Donald Trump, but I didn't always feel that way. He is cocky, boastful—and that hair . . . ! But several years ago I was seated next to him at a tribute to Vietnam veterans at the memorial in downtown Manhattan. Our tablemate was Medal of Honor recipient Paul Bucha, Captain, U.S. Army (Ret.). Melania wasn't there, so I guess Donald had no one to speak with but me. Still, as he spoke, I was stunned. He didn't talk about himself. Instead he discussed the type of bravery shown by the servicemen seated all around us. He wondered why more people didn't see the importance of publicly recognizing the love of country, courage, and selflessness of these veterans.

In the course of the evening Bucha told me that Donald's involvement was a main reason the memorial was finally built. While it's true that Donald makes sure he gets credit for what he does, the fact is that he gets it done when other people don't. He has a right to be proud of what he's accomplished. In business he's made branding an art form. Is it egotistical to put your name on everything? Maybe. But it's also ingenious, because people know that if something has the Trump name on it they can expect it to be top-of-the-line. I've spent more time with Donald since then, and I know that he is generous, witty, and enchanting.

ENJOY WHAT YOU DO

My father was a really smart man who had great wisdom. There were two things he would tell me: First, do what you like to do. Second, never give up—even if what you enjoy is something that won't bring you great wealth. He didn't really teach me by saying things over and over; instead, I watched him and studied him, and learned by following the example he set.

In order to be good at something, my father felt, you had to enjoy it.

That was my father's philosophy. He wouldn't sit down with me and say it out loud, but he showed me.

KNOW YOUR SUBJECT

My father loved his business. He loved what he was doing. He'd work on Saturdays and Sundays. He'd go and inspect construction sites and ask me to go along. It wasn't always my favorite way to spend the weekend, but I could see how much he loved the business and that's why he was good at it.

My father did his business in Brooklyn and Queens. He never wanted to come into Manhattan. He felt it wasn't his territory. He felt you had to know your subject. So in a sense that was good for me, because he wasn't here. I knew he wanted me to follow him in business, and he left that market open for me.

ALWAYS BEAT THE COMPETITION

My father also taught me that you had to be honorable but strong. "Always beat the competition," he told me. I probably took that to the next level. That's why I treat some of the people who compete against me the way I do.

Mark Cuban, the owner of the Dallas Mavericks, tried to duplicate the success of *The Apprentice.* He went after me, but he crashed and burned. So I went after him, and it was easy because he didn't have the "It" factor. He thought he did, but he didn't. The worst are the people who think they have it and don't. Both he and Richard Branson, who started Virgin, had no television persona. Both thought they did, but they were wrong. So, as soon as I watched Cuban's first interview, I realized that his show would fail because I saw what he was like on television.

Even so, if Cuban hadn't taken the first pot shots I would have been fine. But he was doing everything he could to get publicity for himself. I will say this about him: he made one good move. He sold his company stock before it crashed. That was good. You know, some people would say that was lucky. I would say that was smart.

I think I brought a lot of the wackos out of the woods when *The Ap-*

prentice became the number one show on television. Other guys said, "Well, if Trump can do it, maybe we can do it." Now I think I've bought a year or two, because the failure of the first couple of rich guys who challenged me should keep the rest away.

It's interesting how nice they become after they fail. They're nasty at the beginning, before they start; they get nastier as the competition goes along; and then, when they fail, they write you a nice letter saying that we shouldn't be criticizing each other. It's really interesting what happens when you beat the competition.

President Gerald Ford and Sandy Weill

SANDY WEILL

CEO OF CITIGROUP

Most people don't know the Sandy Weill I know. Sandy is a business legend. He began with nothing. In 1955 he made his first fortuitous acquisition when he proposed to his wife, Joan, whose intelligence, strength, and love can't be understated when evaluating what Sandy's accomplished. His first firm, Carter, Berlind & Weill, formed in 1960, grew into the second largest securities brokerage firm by 1979, when after a series of mergers it became Shearson Loeb Rhoades. That soon was sold to American Express, where he became president.

In 1985 he quit AmEx and started over with Commercial Credit, a consumer finance company. Over the next years, Gulf Insurance, Primerica, Smith Barney, Shearson Lehman, Travelers Corp., Aetna, and Salomon Inc. all merged with his company. Eventually, in 1998, his efforts culminated with a historic $76 billion merger with Citicorp. The company that resulted was renamed Citigroup, with more than 100 million customers in more than 100 countries.

That's the business side of Sandy. Here's my side: Sandy is one of the most ethical and charitable people I've ever known. Ever since I met him in 1987, I have watched Sandy take the high road in everything he does. Both Sandy and Joan are life role models for all of my children. They teach them honesty, compassion, empathy, and determination.

STUDY YOUR SUBJECT

Right after World War II, my parents moved from Florida back to New York. There was a housing shortage, and I wasn't doing well in high school because I really didn't have any discipline in my studies. So my parents decided to send me off to Peekskill Military Academy in Peekskill, New York.

I had been doing so poorly that I was put back a half grade. I started playing tennis, and really grew to like the tennis coach, Clare Franz. He came from Lancaster, Pennsylvania, and had taught at Franklin & Marshall, a local college. Coach Franz and his wife lived on campus, and I developed a close relationship with both of them and spent a lot of time at their house. Coach Franz also taught the Latin class. Because of my respect for him, I really started to study for all my classes.

Latin is a language of logic. It's not like learning to speak French or German. It makes sense. Coach Franz told me, "If you are disciplined studying Latin, it will begin to make sense. It's the same with tennis." He was right on both counts. You could study your opponents' games and figure out their style. My tennis coach had a tremendous influence on my life. Because of him, I was a better tennis player and a better person.

LEARN TO TAKE THE PUNISHMENT BEFORE GIVING IT OUT

I really enjoyed the structure of military school. As a plebe, you learn to take a lot of hazing. People go out of their way to make it hard on you. So when it was my turn to start handing it out, I'd learned to be a little more thoughtful. You learn to take the punishment before you start dishing it out.

I ended up loving the experience, even though it was very tough at the beginning. I became an officer, and played bass drum in the band. Two times, a German shepherd bit through my white duck shoes because he didn't like the sound of my bass drum. That band experience was the background for my later involvement in work on behalf of Carnegie Hall. But band wasn't the only thing I spent my time on: By the end of my senior year I was one of the top tennis players in the region, and I'd been accepted into both Cornell for engineering and Harvard for liberal arts. It was the time of *Sputnik*, so I decided to be an engineer.

I learned discipline and logic in high school; only later did I learn to be a dreamer.

THINK CREATIVELY

One man who influenced me greatly was Sonny Werblin. At that time, the future of the AFL was pretty shaky. The New York AFL team, the Titans, was having trouble drawing a crowd, whereas the NFL's New York Giants went to the NFL Championship game four times in six years. A group of investors, led by Werblin—who'd been an agent with MCA and was a great promoter—stepped up and bought the Titans for one million dollars. The next year, they moved the team into a new stadium near LaGuardia Airport and changed their name to the Jets. Then Werblin really shook things up, laying out $427,000—which was big money at the time—to sign Joe Namath, who was one of the top pro prospects in the nation. Concerned that the AFL would start grabbing up other big name players, the NFL offered a common draft and agreed to play a championship game. I was brought in to do some real estate investing for Joe Namath, and I got to know all the players on the team. Werblin was always thinking creatively; in my mind, he's the guy who saved the AFL. He knew how to dream.

DARE TO DREAM

My own dreaming continued when I met Isaac Stern, who set an example for decades. In the late 1950s, when developers wanted to tear down Carnegie Hall to build another high-rise, Isaac organized an opposition movement within the music community, and against great odds the city was able to buy the building and lease it to a nonprofit organization. Isaac truly saved that venerable world institution from the wrecker's ball. Then, in the early 1980s, when Carnegie Hall needed an extensive makeover, Isaac dreamed big once again. The result was an exquisite renovation. It was a wonderful experience working with him, and I gained such respect for Isaac in the process. He taught me that you should dare to dream, whatever events were swirling around you.

In 1991, during the first Gulf War, Isaac was in Israel playing with the Israeli Philharmonic. Suddenly, in the middle of Mozart's 3rd Violin Concerto, the air raid sirens began to wail. The orchestra disappeared. Everyone, in their finest evening wear, put on their gas masks—everyone but Isaac. He stayed there on the stage, breathing freely, and continued to play. He was a great example of leadership. Numerous times I let Isaac know how much he affected my life. Unfortunately, I never told my tennis coach. Later in life I tried to find him, but I was never able to. I have said thank you to him many times in my heart, and I hope he can hear me.

HENRY WINKLER

ACTOR

It's not often that you find actors with Ph.D.s! Then again, Henry Winkler isn't your ordinary actor. He started out on Broadway and in films like The Lords of Flatbush, *but soon he was taking television by storm. No one can forget the memorable role he created as Arthur "Fonzie" Fonzarelli on the sitcom* Happy Days. *He took what was intended to be a minor role and managed to make it a starring role by the end of the show's ten-year run. When I was growing up, every kid I knew was repeating Fonzie's catchphrases "Aaaay" and "Sit on it!" There were Fonzie posters, Fonzie dolls, even Fonzie novels! It was a one-man industry.*

After Happy Days *went into reruns, Henry started working behind the camera, while also appearing in television shows such as* Arrested Development *and* Law & Order, *and movies such as* Scream, The Waterboy, Down to You, *and more. He earned producer credits on the series* MacGyver *and the movie* Mr. Sunshine, *and he's directed several movies including* Memories of Me *and* Cop and a Half. *Off screen, Henry is a vociferous advocate for charities that benefit underprivileged children.*

PASS ON WHAT YOU DISCOVER

I never got any great advice, although I wish I had. Here's one piece of advice I do think is worth sharing: I would tell people that it's mandatory that we pass on what we know. No matter how the younger generation may present themselves to the world, they are eager sponges. They all want to know if there are rules, or answers, or shortcuts that will help them get where they want to go and get what they want from life. I think it's our responsibility—if we're asked and sometimes even when we're not—to pass on what we have discovered along the way.

I, for one, have found that there are no shortcuts. You may try to take a shortcut, but when you do you spend a lot of time going right back down the road to get onto the main highway again.

PREPARE YOURSELF, EDUCATE YOURSELF, AND THEN BE TENACIOUS

For me, an incredibly important word is "tenacity." You must be tenacious. Find your own personal power, and make sure you use it. What is it that will get you from where you are to where you want to be? It's tenacity, coupled with an education. After the incredible success of *Happy Days,* I had tremendously good times and great opportunities. I met wonderful people. But I also came face-to-face with a thing called typecasting. The Fonz was such a huge character that it was very difficult to keep the ball rolling in a different direction. So I had to be tenacious and create my own world. With the help of my lawyer I started producing, and then I started directing. I didn't really know how to do those things at first, but I realized that the anticipatory fear of starting something new was worse than actually just doing it.

MAKE A DIFFERENCE IN SOMEONE'S LIFE

I don't think that anything in life is serendipitous. I loved the development of the Fonz. He was my great alter ego, because he was everybody I wanted to be. But when you achieve success, you can fall in the trap of starting to believe that you are better or more important than everyone else. But you have to remember that you're still the same human being. The best way to use success is to try to make a difference in other people's lives. You don't always know if you're going to succeed, but it's always worth trying. I think that high-profile people need to use their celebrity status to try to bring brightness into others' lives.

THE ENERGY YOU PUT OUT
IS THE ENERGY YOU GET BACK

Gratitude is another cornerstone of life. I love the pleasure of being alive. I'm really fortunate. I tell my children, "The energy you put out is the energy you get back." I repeat that probably six or seven million times a year. And I'll tell you what's amazing: whether or not your own children ever allow you the pleasure of knowing that your advice is making an impact on their lives, eventually you see it—when you notice that they're doing something you suggested . . . and your heart sings.

E. D. fishing with her daughter and father, 1995

E. D. HILL

HOST OF FOX'S MORNING NEWS SHOW
FOX AND FRIENDS

★ ★ ★

Even if you spend your career in front of the camera and in front of people, there's often a wall between yourself and your viewers. When I was covering local news in Duluth, Waco, Pittsburgh, Boston, and New York, I always thought it was inappropriate to interject my own feelings into a story. That was difficult, especially when I was covering stories involving abused or neglected children or serial criminals.

In particular, I was frustrated and disappointed when I would cover a crime in a destitute area and the neighbors would protect the criminal and create fictitious stories about excessive police force. You've all heard it happen, when some relative of a suspect says, "The police are after the wrong person. They're just picking on him because he's black," or yellow, or pink, or whatever color they might be. "Why are they hassling boys in our neighborhood? They're good boys. Leave them alone." Instead, they should be saying, "There's the guy who robbed this store. Lock him up and let's make this a better, safer place for the rest of the kids." Over and over, people allow their neighborhoods to be terrorized by thwarting police attempts to help. Of course, at neighborhood meetings the very same people then talk about how the police had neglected the area.

For me, the worst part of working in local news was watching, day in and day out, as people refused to take responsibility for themselves or their surroundings.

BE ABLE TO STAND ON YOUR OWN

Early in my life, my mother taught me responsibility and self-reliance. She'd say, "You should be able to do everything for yourself, so you won't have to rely on anyone for anything. You should have a job, so you won't need anyone to take care of you. Be able to stand on your own." I recall learning how

to change brake pads in a car before I even had a driver's license! After I got
a car, I learned how to change the oil and repair the tires. At home, I learned
how to rewire lamps, finds studs, install molding, lay brick, snake sinks,
build fences, and take apart and put together vacuum cleaners. You name it,
I learned to do it. My siblings did the same.

That early training served me well when I started working—and my
salary was so low I qualified for help from the food bank. Fortunately, I
didn't need to use the service because I'd learned to be frugal . . . and how to
fish. I figured out what foods went the farthest, shopped the grocery store
specials, and became adept at making breakfast, lunch, and dinner from tor-
tillas, eggs, ground beef, lettuce, cheese, and peppers, which were the staples
in my refrigerator. In the summer, friends and I would catch fish on the
weekends. I also looked forward to my parents' visits. My mom would make
beef stroganoff and chicken chow mein until my freezer was stuffed. They'd
bring big party platters of food to the TV station, and everyone would take
food home. It was difficult making ends meet, but it was also comforting to
learn that I could really get by with very little and be quite happy.

There is a downside to being so self-reliant, though: I found it very difficult ever to let anyone help me. And if they tried but couldn't do it as well
as I could, I was disappointed. When something was broken, my husband
usually wasn't able to fix it, and chances were I could. That often left me
frustrated, because I also wanted a traditional marriage where the man does
the manly things. Unfortunately, I'd jump in and do them before he got the
chance to or because I could do it better . . . then I'd get mad at him! Yet I
couldn't stop myself from proving that I didn't need him to do things for
me. It was the same thing with the babies. Since I knew how to do the guy
things, I figured, my husband should know how to do girl things—how to
interpret cries, to fix a bottle, to bathe, feed, clothe, and soothe the children.
If he couldn't do these things well, I felt I was being the husband *and* the
wife, and it wasn't fair.

Needless to say, this power struggle, along with other issues, put a big
strain on our relationship, and he is now my ex. To his credit, I can now admit he sometimes had a point when he would say, "Being able to fix something doesn't mean you always should." I recall hearing that line specifically

after an electrical shock blew me off a ladder while I was attempting to rewire a light in a dark hallway!

My husband, Mr. Hill, is a Texan. According to him, that means he knows he's the man and doesn't need to prove it. So he'll tell me he can fix something if I want him to, but he's also fine if I want to do it myself.

MAKE THE WORLD A BETTER PLACE

My father changed my life when he told me, "If you leave this earth without having made it a better place, you never really lived, you just took." My parents are tough acts to follow. They helped found the first library in my town. My parents were both very involved members of the school board. Dad volunteered to drive the school bus, Mom served as a substitute teacher, they led Boy Scout and Girl Scout troops, and were poll volunteers during elections. When natural disasters occurred around the country, they'd grab a sleeping bag and hop on a bus to go help. They traveled overseas to build homes for the poor. They volunteered for the Peace Corps. They never said no to anyone in need.

It's still almost impossible for me to speak about my dad. As I write this it's about 5:30 A.M. There are some robins hopping on the lawn outside my window, and a blue jay has made his home in a tree nearby. Dad taught me to love nature, and we spent a great deal of time together out fishing on the lake. I don't think there's a more wonderful experience you can share with a child than to go fishing. Out there in the middle of a lake or stream, there's time to learn, talk, and reflect. Dad taught me to bait my hook, cast, read the banks, tie flies, fly fish, and run a boat. As crazy as it may sound, we had in-depth discussions about God's amazing creations: the countless varieties of daffodils; how to tell a red pine needle from a white (red pine needles have two needles in a fascicle; white pines have three to five needles apiece); where and how to find edible berries in a forest; and much, much more.

Dad called this kind of talk sharing "bits and pieces of worthless information," but he knew it was more than that. When he was driving the school bus, he made the children learn the name of every creek, tree, and plant they passed on the thirty-mile ride to school. As a pilot for TWA, he was infamous for naming (on the loudspeaker) each body of water, including rivers, his plane flew over. He was a tremendous human being. He died six years ago and not a day goes by when I don't wish I could call him. I want to let him know that I'm trying to follow his advice through my job. I'm helping inform people so they can make better decisions for themselves and for our country. I hope that through the advice compiled in this book people will take away something that improves them.

DON'T CHEAT YOURSELF

The other advice that changed my life came from my high school biology teacher, Becky Huffman. The very fact that she actually became my teacher is a miracle. Each semester, starting in my freshman year, I would sign up for biology. But the school was so small that there was only one biology teacher, and time and again I dropped the class after the first day—because Mrs. Huffman scared me.

Where every other teacher was nice and patient, Mrs. Huffman was no-nonsense. She made it very clear that no amount of smiling or sucking up was going to work in her class. She expected me to work to my own potential. That was something entirely new to me. I was never a straight-A student. I had always skated through classes, getting mostly B's without much studying. She was the first person who wouldn't let me get away with that. For whatever reason, she knew I wasn't trying very hard in school, and she was determined to change that. And for the next three years I slipped out of her grasp.

Finally, when my senior year came along, I had no choice: I had to take her class in order to graduate. That first day she grinned from ear to ear, because she knew I couldn't escape. When I'd turn in my usual so-so work, she'd keep me after class and tell me she expected more. "You can get by doing the bare minimum," she told me, "but you won't get the maximum out of life." She was right. The only way to get her off my back was to study— and it turned out that the more I studied, the more I enjoyed the class. She became one of the dearest people in my life.

In college I didn't always feel challenged, and I began to let my grades slip. Then I ran into Professor Don Ostrowsky at Harvard. I turned in my first paper to him, and was shocked to get it back without a grade. When I asked why, he told me it didn't have a grade because it wasn't worthy of one! Needless to say, I shaped up.

As Mrs. Huffman said, anyone can do the bare minimum and get by— at work, at school, or in relationships. If you fail to carry your own weight, you won't get promoted, you won't get into college or graduate school, and you won't maintain healthy relationships with friends and family. In essence, if you don't give it your all and be fully committed, you'll never be truly successful in anything you do.

It was a hard lesson to learn, but for me it's been worth it.

ACKNOWLEDGMENTS

Thank you Adrienne and Ron Hay. Your hard work, countless hours, and ceaseless fact checking, while simultaneously welcoming your sixth child into the world, made this book possible. Thanks to my brother, Dr. Grant Tarbox, and his wife, Lori, for putting up with crazy sisters. Also, thank you Roger Ailes, Mike Sechrist, Jacques Natz, and Ron Lund for believing in me.